Heather Raffo's Iraq Plays:
The Things That Can't Be Said

Heather Raffo's Iraq Plays: The Things That Can't Be Said

9 Parts of Desire; *Fallujah*; *Noura*

Edited with Introduction by
MICHAEL MALEK NAJJAR

methuen | drama
LONDON • NEW YORK • OXFORD • NEW DELHI • SYDNEY

METHUEN DRAMA
Bloomsbury Publishing Plc
50 Bedford Square, London, WC1B 3DP, UK
1385 Broadway, New York, NY 10018, USA

BLOOMSBURY, METHUEN DRAMA and the Methuen Drama logo are trademarks of
Bloomsbury Publishing Plc

First published in Great Britain 2021
Introduction copyright © Michael Malek Najjar, 2021
9 Parts of Desire copyright © Raffo Inc. 2004
Published by arrangement with Heather Raffo. All rights reserved.
Fallujah copyright © Raffo Inc. 2016
Published by arrangement with Heather Raffo. All rights reserved.
Noura copyright © Raffo Inc. 2018
Published by arrangement with Heather Raffo. All rights reserved.
Afterword copyright © Heather Raffo, 2021

Heather Raffo and Michael Malek Najjar have asserted their right under the Copyright, Designs and Patents Act, 1988, to be identified as authors of this work.

For legal purposes the Acknowledgments on p. ix constitute an extension of this copyright page.

Cover design: Louise Dugdale
Cover image © Jeff Rogers

All rights reserved. No part of this publication may be reproduced or transmitted in any form or by any means, electronic or mechanical, including photocopying, recording, or any information storage or retrieval system, without prior permission in writing from the publishers.

Bloomsbury Publishing Plc does not have any control over, or responsibility for, any third-party websites referred to or in this book. All internet addresses given in this book were correct at the time of going to press. The author and publisher regret any inconvenience caused if addresses have changed or sites have ceased to exist, but can accept no responsibility for any such changes.

No rights in incidental music or songs contained in the work are hereby granted and performance rights for any performance/presentation whatsoever must be obtained from the respective copyright owners.

All inquiries regarding the performance of the plays must be addressed to The Gersh Agency, 41 Madison Avenue, 29th Floor, New York, NY 10010, attn: Leah Hamos, (212) 634-8153.

A catalogue record for this book is available from the British Library.

A catalog record for this book is available from the Library of Congress.

ISBN: HB: 978-1-3501-4516-0
PB: 978-1-3501-4517-7
ePDF: 978-1-3501-4518-4
eBook: 978-1-3501-4519-1

Typeset by RefineCatch Limited, Bungay, Suffolk

To find out more about our authors and books visit www.bloomsbury.com and sign up for our newsletters.

*For my father
who in his life and passing taught me how
to let go and hold on at the same time.*

Contents

Foreword by Joanna Settle, Director   viii

Acknowledgments   ix

Introduction by Michael Malek Najjar   1

The Plays

9 Parts of Desire   11

Fallujah   59

Noura   91

Glossary of Arabic Terms and Phrases   149

Afterword: "The Things That Can't Be Said" by Heather Raffo   153

Critical Essay: "Listening to the Soul of Rupture—and Difference in Heather Raffo's Iraqi-American Trilogy" by Dr. Maya Roth, Della Rosa Term Associate Professor of Theater, Georgetown University   159

Annotated Timeline of the Life and Works of Heather Raffo   165

Bibliography   169

Foreword

In 2003, I received a script from Dave Fishelson of Manhattan Ensemble Theater. He'd been given my name by Celise Kalke, then at The Public Theater in New York City. So, one morning I found myself opening an email attachment from a man I didn't know titled simply "9 Parts."

I remember clearly reading that script for the first time. Discovering its uncompromising poetry and elusive rhythms, I sat bolt upright as I read it twice through. Here was the voice of a woman my age howling into the night, demanding space for logic and priorities that women too often keep to ourselves. I recognized then what I celebrate now. Heather creates windows for her audience, revealing psychological interiors. She invites us in as friends.

When we met in 2004 to start rehearsals for *9 Parts of Desire*, Heather was dating a man named Matt. I was newly married. In the first week of rehearsals, I discovered I was pregnant with my son, Logan—born the night we closed our extended off-Broadway run. Together, Heather and I brought *9 Parts* around the country, and it has since gone on its own around the world. For the first year and a half of Logan's life, he was never in one place for more than five weeks.

Other shared projects followed: a workshop of *Fallujah* at the Kennedy Center and our premiere production of *Noura*. A lot of life passed, too: I divorced. Heather married Matt and had two children. As colleagues and friends (truly, sisters at this point), we've helped each other through endless conundrums of mothering, love, and artmaking. I can get her kids to take their medicine, and she serves as a devoted godmother to Logan. When I was diagnosed with breast cancer, she appeared on my doorstep, seemingly to stare at me while I slept.

I share these personal stories to suggest that, as artists, our value might be embedded within our openness. The bile rising around the globe seems to be pushing us further apart, further away from reaching out to our neighbors, further from being entirely ourselves in public. Heather's writing brings us closer. She doesn't solve our problems, but she helps us feel less alone with them. She sneaks up on us, with her poetry and her big brain, until we are unexpectedly "open."

I'm happy you are here, that you have found this collection in your hands. Happy for the concepts, contradictions, and heart you are about to encounter in Heather's work.

As I write this, Logan and I are living under COVID-19 quarantine in Abu Dhabi, with so much of humanity's future uncertain. But one thing I know is that later, in the still-hazy future when I read this foreword in the published book, Heather Raffo's writing will be on my shelf and in my heart. Hopefully, I'll never see the end of her emails in my inbox titled "New Draft."

Joanna Settle
Director

Acknowledgments

Heather Raffo

I would like to thank the countless people whose personal stories gave life to these plays. Without sharing in such deep and truthful ways, works like these would not be possible.

A profound thanks to my collaborators at Georgetown University, especially Maya Roth and Derek Goldman, whose crucial support both dramaturgically and through the Laboratory for Global Performance and Politics offered an artistic lifeline critical to building this work and envisioning a career as a playwright. Thanks to Ron Russell and all at Epic Theater Ensemble who expanded my theatrical landscape of what's possible not only with community, but in community. And to the women of Queens College in New York, whose participation in the Places of Pilgrimage workshop began a movement within me too.

A special thanks to the McCarter Theater at Princeton, especially Emily Mann; Andrea Assaf at Art2Action, Adam Greenfield at Playwrights Horizons, Noor Theater, the Arab American National Museum, and Alicia Adams at the Kennedy Center, for offering readings, residencies, and a sounding board when I most needed to be in conversation. Thanks always to Joanna Settle for her visionary partnership across all three projects; to Tobin Stokes for the inspiration and power of his music; to Caitlin Cassidy, Ni Casey, Alyaa Nasser, Leah Hamos, and Antje Oegel, for years of personal and professional collaboration. Thanks to the Doris Duke Foundation, City Opera Vancouver, and Charlie Annenberg's Explore Foundation for funding process over product. And to the many actors, musicians, and creative teams who participated in developmental workshops, giving tremendously of their talents.

I would like to acknowledge the countless artists, technicians, crews, staff, producers, boards of directors, volunteers, donors, journalists, students, academics, audiences, professional theaters, community theaters, university theaters, and international theaters who have contributed to the conversation and impact of these plays. Without your combined efforts this anthology would not have come into being. To the publishers for embracing this work and most especially to Malek Najjar, whose ability to both document and propel what is now a Middle Eastern American theater movement is peerless.

Thank you, Matt Wells, for holding all three of these journeys as you hold me. Lastly, to all my family, both American and Iraqi, whose history is the true inspiration for this work and to my children for being the bearers and hope of our history to come.

Michael Malek Najjar

First, let me offer my profound thanks to the incomparable Heather Raffo for agreeing to allow me to edit this important collection, and for traveling to both UCLA and the University of Oregon over the years for productions and workshops. Also, thank you for being so open to the many personal questions I have asked of you, and for your willingness to share your story and your plays with me. I speak for many in our Middle Eastern American community when I say that your plays and performances are an inspiration to us all.

Special thanks to Dom O'Hanlon, Meredith Benson, and the excellent staff at Methuen Drama. You have made this process an absolute delight. I would also like to thank the amazing contributors to this book: Joanna Settle, Maya Roth, and Jeff Rogers. Thanks, Joanna, for your inspired directorial vision bringing Heather's plays to the stage over the years; thank you, Maya, for your critical insights into these plays; and thanks, Jeff, for sharing your beautiful cover art.

I would like to acknowledge the theater companies, boards of directors, donors, producers, directors, actors, designers, technicians, stage crews, photographers, dramaturgs, public relations and office staff, and volunteers of the theaters who have produced Heather Raffo's plays these past decades. Without your combined efforts, works like these could not have been staged and shared with audiences nationwide. I would also like to acknowledge the publishers who print plays like these, allowing them to be taught in classrooms, read in libraries, and produced in regional theaters.

I would like to extend special thanks to the Oregon Humanities Center for their support through the 2019–20 Ernest G. Moll Professorship in Literary Studies and the faculty of the University of Oregon Department of Theater.

Lastly, to my extraordinary wife Rana and my precious daughter Malak: I love you always and forever.

Introduction

Michael Malek Najjar

How does an Iraqi American, born and raised in Michigan, address through her art a subject as vast and complicated as contemporary Iraqi history? This was the task Heather Raffo set for herself when she first embarked on writing her seminal play *9 Parts of Desire*, and the terrain she continued to traverse in her later works *Fallujah* and *Noura*. As a formally trained actress, she could have easily made her way into mainstream American theater solely performing in classical dramas. However, the formative trips she took to her father's homeland of Iraq as a child and as a young adult forever shaped her life as a woman, as a performing artist, and as an American citizen. Like many other Americans of Middle Eastern descent, Raffo opposed the Iraq War. Like other Iraqi Americans, she was against Saddam Hussein's brutal regime, yet she did not advocate a violent regime change as a solution. This terrible dichotomy lies at the heart of much Arab American writing, and Raffo's work is no exception. She not only wrote, but also performed, her one-woman show as a complicated and intricate portrait of American interventions in Iraq in an attempt "to create profound context and interwoven humanity" meant to help American audiences see the complexity of the situation there (Najjar, personal interview, 2020).

Raffo's works humanize Iraqi civilians who persevered through dictatorships, the Iran–Iraq War, the First and Second Gulf Wars, the catastrophic aftermath of the U.S. "pullout" of troops (despite building and staffing one of the world's largest U.S. embassies in Baghdad with thousands of employees and contractors).[1] The years following the troop withdrawal and the subsequent power vacuum left behind led to an ongoing U.S. military presence, a rise in ISIS terrorism, greater loss of minority communities, countless drone strikes, and deteriorating living conditions for many Iraqis today. Of course, the greatest toll has been on the Iraqi civilians and the American troops who suffer from post-traumatic stress disorders and moral injuries.[2] Raffo's ability to write so acutely and humanely about the cost of war on both sides of this conflict demonstrates her ability to see past politics, and to focus on the human suffering and resilience that always accompanies wars, occupations, and insurgencies.

Raffo's Iraqi heritage

To understand *9 Parts of Desire*, *Fallujah*, and *Noura*, one must understand Raffo's historic and religious connection to Iraq. Raffo's father, an Iraqi Christian, came from

---

1. Woolf, Christopher. "Whatever Happened to the Giant US Embassy in Baghdad." Pri.org. January 16, 2018. https://www.pri.org/stories/2018-01-16/whatever-happened-giant-us-embassy-baghdad.
2. For more information about these conditions in relation to Iraqi civilians and American soldiers, see Litz, Stein, Delaney, Lebowitz, Nash, Silva, and Maguen. "Moral Injury and Moral Repair in War Veterans: A Preliminary Model and Intervention Strategy." *Clinical Psychology Review* 29, no. 8 (2009): 695–706 and Orkideh Behrouzan, "The Psychological Impact of the Iraq War." ForeignPolicy.com, April 23, 2013. https://foreignpolicy.com/2013/04/23/the-psychological-impact-of-the-iraq-war/#

an ancient city located on the west bank of the Tigris River opposite the ancient city of Nineveh. Mosul is the historic homeland for Arabs, Kurds, Assyrians, Armenians, Turkmens, Shabaks, Jews, Yazidis, Mandeans, Kawliyas, and Circassians. A significant center during the early Islamic period with a large Christian population, the city was later destroyed by the Mongols. During the First Crusade, Mosul became a major staging ground for the Muslim resistance. As part of the Ottoman Empire, it was the capital of an Ottoman province that covered northern Iraq. In the late nineteenth century, the city's population was estimated at forty thousand, including seven thousand Christians and fifteen hundred Jews. After the breakup of the Ottoman Empire following the First World War, the British Army marched into Mosul in 1918, ending Turkish rule in Iraq with the goal of controlling Mosul's oil reserves.

The Iraqi state we know today was created in 1921 from the amalgamation of three defunct Ottoman provinces: Baghdad, Basra, and Mosul. The 1940s and 1950s were prosperous times for the city of Mosul. After oil was discovered there, and a refinery was constructed, Mosul became an important center of power in Iraq. However, a mutiny by Arab Sunnis in 1959 led to the death of hundreds of people. In 1968 the Ba'ath Party seized power in Iraq, and by 1979 Saddam Hussein had eliminated his rivals to become president with imperious authority over the nation. After the ravages of the Iran–Iraq War (1980–88), the Gulf War (1991), and the post-Gulf War sanctions, Hussein elevated Iraq's Sunni Arabist identity above all others.[3] The mounting tensions with the United States following the First Gulf War led to a U.S. invasion in 2003. According to the website Iraq Body Count, since the end of that war there have been between 184,868 and 207,759 documented civilian deaths from violence (iraqbodycount.org). By 2004, the population of Mosul was estimated at 1,846,500 with the population consisting of a Muslim Arab majority and a significant Kurdish, Turkmen, Shabak, and Yazidi minority (Simon 2004; Al-Obeidi 2017).

Calamity struck again in 2014 when ISIS led its campaign to take Mosul. Purges of anti-ISIS forces took place, and the letter "N" for Nazarene was spray painted on homes and shops owned by Christians who were told to either convert, pay a tax, or leave the city with nothing. Many Christians were taken hostage, enslaved, and killed. Other minorities (such as the Shabaks and Yazidis) also fled or were killed. Women were forced to wear the *niqab* and men and women were forbidden to comingle (Abdul-Ahad 2018). Medicine was scarce and many died. Taxation increased, brutal punishments were regularly meted, and ISIS tightened its grip on the population by terrorizing them. In 2017 an all-out military offensive was launched by Iraqi forces backed by coalition forces to liberate the city. According to *The Atlantic*, it is estimated that the U.S.-led coalition that recaptured Mosul left 9,000 to 11,000 civilians killed in the battle, 11 million tons of debris, and an estimated $700 million worth of damages (Coles 2019). Since that time reconstruction has been slow, ISIS has resurged, and conditions are still desperate with fears the growing discontent may breed a new generation of disaffected Iraqis (middleeasteye.net).

Raffo states that her Chaldean Christian grandfathers helped carve Mosul's churches out of marble. That community, which predates Christ, was among the first in the world

---

3. Dawisha, Adeed. "'Identity' and Political Survival in Saddam's Iraq." *Middle East Journal*, Vol. 53, No. 4 (Autumn, 1999): 556.

to convert to Christianity. The Christians in Mosul and the surrounding villages speak an ancient dialect of Aramaic. Raffo's historic Christian community is connected to a 2,000-year-old history in a country that seemingly has no place for them any longer. Raffo says, "My family is scattered across the world. Yet through the war, because of my family's strong connection to the country, I felt I had an identity that would still be part of the fabric of the place," she says. "I feel now that much of that identity is being abandoned; many of my links are being severed" ("Playwright's Perspective" 2011). Iraq's rich pluralistic society has forever changed.

The formative years and *9 Parts of Desire*

Raffo's mother, Lynne, who is of Irish German descent, was born in Battle Creek, Michigan. Raffo's Iraqi father, George, who was born in Mosul to a family of nine, later moved his entire family from Mosul to Baghdad during his undergraduate years. After living in Baghdad for a time, he later immigrated to the U.S. in the 1960s to study at university, and achieved his master's degree in civil engineering. Raffo's parents, both Catholics, were married in 1967. Her father worked for the State of Michigan Highway Department as an engineer, and her mother worked as a high school art teacher. Raffo and her brother David were born in Okemos, Michigan (he in 1968, and Heather Raffo in 1970). Her first trip to Iraq with her family was in 1974. During that trip she recalls sleeping on the roof under the stars, watching her uncle care for and fly his pigeons, and visiting Babylon. From a child's perspective, she fell in love with Iraq: its desert, the passionate people she met, and the endless food and parties (Najjar, personal interview, 2020).

For her undergraduate education, she enrolled at the University of Michigan, and she graduated with her Bachelor of Arts in Literature in 1992. She then moved to London for six months, traveled around Europe, and in 1993, Raffo made what she called a "life-changing trip" to Iraq, where she met her father's extended family, this time as an adult. Her journey to Iraq that year was a crucial event in the formation of *9 Parts of Desire.* "I was like an orphan finding her family on that trip," she wrote, "soaking up every story about their lives and how my father grew up" (Raffo 2006, ix). She saw buildings her grandfather and great-grandfather built, visited her father's childhood home, toured the Amirlyya bomb shelter, and visited the Saddam Art Center in Baghdad where she saw the haunting painting *Savagery* by the artist Layla Al-Attar; a painting that would serve as a central image in her play *9 Parts of Desire*. She also spoke with many Iraqi women at that time.

> They shared so deeply of themselves and seemed to tell me almost anything, but only after I shared as much of myself with them. My process was not one of formal interviews but rather a process of spending time together living, eating, communicating compassionately, and loving on such a level that when I parted from their homes it was clear to all that we were now family. When an Iraqi woman trusts you, it is because she has come to love you, and that has been the process of finding and forming these stories.
>
> (Raffo 2006, x)

After moving back to New York City in 1994, Raffo intended to start work as a professional actress. She applied to the Royal Academy of Dramatic Art (RADA) Shakespeare Summer School in 1995. At RADA she found a "deep understanding and commitment to Shakespeare," adding, "I cannot underestimate the influence of Shakespeare on my call to becoming a writer" (Najjar, personal interview, 2020). In the works of Shakespeare, she found great admiration for density of the text and language, and the strength of the female characters. In the fall of 1996 she applied for, and was accepted to, the University of San Diego/the Old Globe for her MFA in Acting. It was there she began writing her thesis, what would ultimately become *9 Parts of Desire*. She graduated from the Old Globe and University of San Diego Shiley Graduate Theatre program in 1998.

In 1999 she moved back to New York City to pursue a professional career as an actor. She was cast in the off-Broadway run of *Over the River and Through the Woods* and she toured playing Lady Macbeth with The Acting Company. With the election of George W. Bush in 2000, Raffo distinctly remembers telling her father that the U.S. would be going to war with Iraq once more. She engaged more deeply in researching and writing *9 Parts of Desire*, despite not finding a home to develop the piece. During this time she recalls feeling isolated, dealing with the frustrations she had developing the play and the inevitability of the U.S. invasion of Iraq. However, she believed that, in the right hands, the play could have a powerful impact.

Initially Raffo was not drawn to the genre of solo performance and was not naturally inclined to write it. For her, *9 Parts of Desire* was more about telling a story in a structure that "heightens what is being said," and finding a form that matched the function of the collected consciousness and spirit of one person playing nine Iraqi women in what she calls "a psychic civil war on stage" (Najjar, personal interview, 2010). The play required a solo performance structure only because the story she was telling required one person to inhabit nine different lives. For Raffo, *9 Parts of Desire* is more a play than a solo performance—or in her words, a combination of "storytelling, performance art, and a play." Raffo's assessment of her own work is confirmed by the fact that the play has been performed successfully both as a solo performance and with several actresses playing the various roles.

Raffo believes her *9 Parts of Desire* is autobiographical in the same way that a play like *A Streetcar Named Desire* is considered autobiographical (Najjar, personal interview, 2010). The play is not documentary theater where subject testimonies are recorded and performed verbatim (such as *The Laramie Project* or *Fires in the Mirror: Crown Heights, Brooklyn, and Other Identities*), but rather it is a poetic collage (in the vein of Ntozake Shange's *for colored girls who have considered suicide / when the rainbow is enuf*) of the lives and stories of Iraqi women. The audience sometimes imposes autobiography upon Raffo, especially with the character named "The American," who Raffo states is not meant to represent her, although it draws from her life. Instead of accepting the term "autobiographical," Raffo prefers to think of the piece as deeply personal. Raffo is clear that, "with rare exception, these stories are not told verbatim. Most are composites, and although each character is based in fact and research, I consider all the women in my play to be dramatized characters in a poetic story" (Raffo, 2006). Some of the characters are rooted in historical figures while others are not. The most biographical is Huda, drawn heavily from the sculptor Dalal Al Mufti, whom Raffo met and lived with in London. The artist Layal was inspired by the artistic work of the Iraqi painter Layla Al-Attar, who was killed along with her husband and housekeeper when a U.S. bomb destroyed her house in 1993. Umm Ghada was inspired by Umm Greyda, a woman who lost eight children in the U.S. bombing at the Amiriyya Bomb Shelter. The other characters represent different figures in Iraqi society: doctors, children, Bedouins, Iraqi exiles, and Iraqi Americans. The Doctor's monologue about the birth defects caused by use of depleted uranium and white phosphorus is linked to the use of these weapons by coalition forces during the Iraq War (Wilson 2005; Al-Azzawi 2009).

By August 2003, Raffo was performing *9 Parts of Desire* at the Traverse Theatre in Edinburgh, Scotland, directed by Eva Breneman. The play then moved to the Bush Theatre in London, where it was chosen as one of the "Five Best Plays" by *The Independent*. A developmental workshop performance followed at Queens Theater in The Park, directed by Jack Hofsiss. In May 2004, New York's Public Theatre selected the play to be part of their New Work Now reading festival, where it was further developed by director Kate Saxon. In October 2004 *9 Parts of Desire* premiered Off Broadway at the Manhattan Ensemble Theater, directed by Joanna Settle, running for nine months and winning the Lucille Lortel Award, the Susan Smith Blackburn, and Marian Seldes–Garson Kanin playwriting awards. The play was nominated for the Helen Hayes, Outer Critics Circle, and Drama League Awards. It moved to the Geffen Playhouse, Berkeley Rep, Seattle Rep, and Arena Stage before it was licensed nationally and internationally. According to Theatre Communications Group (TCG) it was one of the most produced plays of the 2007–2008 national theater season. Since then, it has been produced hundreds of times both domestically and internationally by professional, semi-professional, and university theaters. Raffo married BBC journalist Matthew Wells in 2007. Raffo was touring *9 Parts of Desire* across the nation at the time, and her marriage was a stabilizing force for her. "I would say much of my marriage was forged in *9 Parts of Desire*," she recounts.

> Because Matt was a BBC journalist at the time, as I traveled doing the show he was able to travel with me working and doing stories from each different location. So instead of my being on the road and Matt being in New York City, he was able to experience how my life was changing and forging in this ongoing conversation around America during the war and occupation. And I was being forged in his work of covering stories in all corners of America. We grew so close. Without him, I simply would not have been able to sustain the pressure, the endurance it takes to do a solo show.
> (Najjar, personal interview, 2020)

The same year she married, Raffo and Iraqi American composer, trumpeter, santur player, and vocalist Amir El Saffar collaborated on a concert version of the piece titled *Sounds of Desire*. She and El Saffar travelled to universities and art centers both nationally and internationally with the work for the following decade.

Raffo was pregnant with her first child, Safia, while performing *9 Parts of Desire* in Chicago with Next Theatre Company at the Museum of Contemporary Art. "She was on stage with me," Raffo recounts, "which was a profound moment. I had already been doing the play for five years. But to be performing with the knowledge that I was becoming a mother, that I was carrying life, infused all the lines with something new"

(Najjar, personal interview, 2020). Her daughter was born a month before her performance of *Sounds of Desire* during the prestigious 2009 Kennedy Center Arabesque: Arts of the Arab World Festival, the first international festival of Arab arts in America after 9/11.

Raffo believes that *9 Parts of Desire* is important because the play asks us to look past our preconceptions and prejudices about Iraqis and to encounter these women and girls as human beings with the same aspirations, difficulties, and desires that all of us share. Raffo adds, "the women in this play are all seeking peace in both their country and within themselves" (Najjar, personal interview 2020). In Raffo's view, empathy building is not enough; instead she calls for plays that create value and allow audiences to see "the other" as equals. Raffo's words help to remind us that there is a common humanity that transcends the politics, borders, and ideologies that separate us. Perhaps, through works like these, we can remember those who never had the opportunity to know a world without war.

Fallujah

While *9 Parts of Desire* was in production in Vancouver, Canada, Raffo was approached by City Opera Vancouver Board President Nora Kelly to write the libretto for an opera based on a scenario by former Marine Sargent Christian Ellis. Ellis served in Fallujah and returned as one of the only survivors of an ambush with a broken back and post-traumatic stress syndrome. *Fallujah* would be the first opera about the Iraq War and the most notable commission in Canadian opera history, funded by Charles Annenberg Weingarten's philanthropic Explore Foundation. In order to begin her process, Raffo met with Ellis in New York for ten-hour days for a week. For Raffo, the opera contends with the American cost of the war on Iraqis, which challenged Raffo to examine the war from a different perspective. In addition to the four workshops with composer Tobin Stokes, provided by City Opera Vancouver over two years, she researched and wrote the libretto while serving as Artist in Residence at Vassar College, and further workshopped the libretto at Georgetown's LAB for Global Performance and Politics. The opera had its first public performance at City Opera Vancouver in 2012. It was then featured in the Kennedy Center's International Theater Festival in 2014 and received developmental support through Art2Action and the Doris Duke Foundation's Building Bridges Grant at the University of Tampa in 2015. The world premiere of *Fallujah* was at Long Beach Opera in 2016, directed by Andreas Mitisek. The production then moved to New York City Opera in November 2016. A live taping of the opera was filmed by KCET and aired on PBS on Veterans Day 2016. A documentary film titled *Fallujah: Art, Healing, and PTSD* was also produced to accompany the opera, funded by the Annenberg Foundation.

For Raffo, taking on this project was difficult. By that time, almost all her family had fled Iraq. Out of a hundred family members, Raffo says only two remain, while the rest are scattered worldwide. She was reticent to re-create Ellis's story as a hero's journey. "I said, well, I'm not the person who can write the hero story. I'm not given toward that. But I can tell you what I think the story is. I think the real story is that it is harder to return than to die in battle" (*Artbound* 2016). Ironically, Raffo found that it was the veterans, and not her fellow non-military civilians, who understood the Iraq War best. "As soon as I get with them, we're talking about the reality. We're talking about how hard it is. They're the only other people in America that actually get it" (Ulaby 2016).

For Raffo, there was a natural connection between her work on *9 Parts of Desire* and *Fallujah*. "Both *9 Parts* and *Fallujah* are poeticized, fictionalized versions of the truth. They're all based in truth but in once sense it's a play and in the other it's an opera. We really make use of theatricality to tell the story" (*Artbound* 2016). The play was not a biography of Ellis; although hugely inspired by her conversations with him. Instead, it was about the difficulty of communicating with loved ones about traumatic experiences and trying to find some way back to an intimate relationship despite surviving something incredibly difficult to communicate. "This opera is meant to be a conversation," Raffo says. "It's meant to be a conversation about somewhat taboo subjects that aren't being talked about openly" (*Artbound* 2016). For her, getting the story "emotionally right" was necessary. She wanted to structure the libretto in such a way that the audience would understand what it was like to experience PTSD. Much of the mother–son relationships found in the opera between the Americans Colleen and Philip, and the Iraqis Shatha and Wissam, came from having just given birth to her own son prior to writing the libretto. Raffo's son, Jasper, was born in 2010, and being a mother to a young boy added a deeper perspective to her writing of *Fallujah*. "A lot of the writing and mothering that came through these two particular mother characters was both from my own psyche at the time, and the various mothers I was speaking to about what it was like to have a grown son in a war zone and the dichotomy of that. Me literally caring for a very young life and mothers feeling such similar things but for grown sons" (*Books and Arts Daily* 2012).

Raffo views the work less politically and more humanistically. "I wanted us all to collectively experience, without a political point of view, how the memory of violence is carried by all who come into contact with it, how hard it is to heal from and how deep is the human desire to communicate even during conflict" (Outman 2012). During the production of the opera, Raffo was looking ahead at the wars' effects on American society. "We're in a period when tens of thousands of U.S. servicemen and women are coming home. That's what the next five years will be about—how we as a nation look after those who had terrible experiences in Iraq and Afghanistan" (Dowd 2012). The next five years led Raffo back to the topic of Iraq, but this time not by exploring Iraqi lives under Saddam or the U.S. military occupation, but rather through the rise of the rise of the so-called "Islamic State," and the fracturing of Iraq's pluralistic identity which has led to the greatest refugee crisis in our time and the deterioration of the Middle East for generations to come.

Noura

Raffo's play *Noura* came about through a Doris Duke Grant working with Epic Theater Ensemble to take her "Places of Pilgrimage" workshop into the Arab American communities of New York. Over a three-year process, Raffo worked closely with refugee, immigrant, and American-born Middle Eastern women on developing their own narratives and writing in response to themes found in Henrik Ibsen's classic play *A Doll's House*. Raffo wrote her own response to Ibsen's play, which ultimately became the play *Noura*. After a decade of performing *9 Parts of Desire*, and traveling around the world speaking about the play, it was once more difficult for Raffo to find a route to production. "So, in a way," she says, "I had to prove myself all over again" (Najjar, personal interview, 2020).

Eventually the play won the Weissberger New Play Award through the Williamstown Theatre Festival which ultimately led to a production. It then received developmental residencies and readings at the McCarter Theater, Williamstown Theatre Festival, Epic Theater Ensemble, Kansas City Repertory Theatre, Classic Stage Company, Noor Theater, and the Arab American National Museum. In January 2018, the play had its world premiere at the Shakespeare Theatre in Washington, D.C. where it won a Helen Hayes/Charles MacArthur Award for Outstanding Original New Play, directed by Joanna Settle, and starring Raffo in the role of Noura. The play then moved to The Arts Center at NYU Abu Dhabi and, in December 2018, had its New York debut at Playwrights Horizons. The 2019–2020 season saw the play programmed in theaters across the nation as well as staged at the American University of Cairo, with Raffo in attendance.

In many ways, *Noura* is Raffo's most personal and harrowing play since it deals with the rise of the so-called "Islamic State" in Mosul, the ancestral homeland of Raffo's Iraqi Christian family. According to research by Aid to the Church in Need (ACN), "within a generation, Iraq's Christians have declined by 90 percent to below 250,000. Some reports suggest that the actual figure may be lower than 120,000" (Pontifex 2020). For Raffo, who watched the destruction of her Christian community in Mosul from afar, the effects were very personal. "A lot of the play came out of listening to family and friends that used to see themselves as Iraqi and then felt that they didn't have an identity there anymore and wanting to create a very personal story about people that feel fractured while they're looking for a sense of wholeness and belonging" ("In Process"). The play also came from personal experiences she had not just as an Arab American, but also as a wife and mother. Raffo sees herself as an "essential bridge" between an American mother and an Iraqi-born father. "I am an artist, a mother, a wife, and an American woman with Middle Eastern heritage. This play came out of the shifting awareness that unfolds when any one of a person's many identities demands growth. As we strive to grow, sometimes one aspect of ourselves calls out above others" ("Playwright's Perspective"). Raffo says the play has been embraced differently by various communities. "*Noura* sits comfortably in the religiously conservative heartland but is also welcomed by young audiences for its bold feminism. Some embrace it solely as a refugee family story, others see it as a provocation, where women do the unforgivable. All seem challenged by the juxtaposition of female ambition and male vulnerability. All seemed connected to the question of how we let go and hold on at the same time" (Najjar, personal interview, 2020).

A play like *Noura*, which has been produced across the United States at major theaters such as the Guthrie Theater in Minneapolis, The Old Globe in San Diego, the Marin Theatre Company in association with Golden Thread Productions, and Detroit Public Theatre, heralds a major step forward in Arab American drama. Raffo has crossed a threshold that few other Arab American playwrights have—namely she has made the story of Middle Eastern lives something embraced by the wider American theater establishment. The play has won several prestigious awards but, most importantly, it has also given American audiences a view into Iraqi and Iraqi American lives they would not have had otherwise. At a time when immigration issues are polarizing American society as never before, this was a necessary humanization of a people terribly dehumanized by the American government and media for over thirty years. In Raffo's work, American theatres are finally able to allow stories about Iraq to be told by Iraqi Americans; something that should have been allowed decades ago.

Bridging Middle Eastern and U.S. cultures

In 2013, Heather Raffo traveled back to Iraq to watch her play *9 Parts of Desire* performed by Iraqi students at the American University of Iraq-Sulaimani. The five-woman cast was comprised of Kurdish and Arab students acting together onstage. Raffo recalled:

> Seeing *9 Parts* in Iraq was a once in a lifetime experience. The students who tackled the production were so brave and powerful. They had to cut almost half the text for it to be safe for them to perform on stage. Yet somehow, it felt they were able to make the unsaid said. They obviously felt a deep connection to the material and understood its intricacies. Most of them were about the age of the Iraqi Girl when the war broke out. So they lived through a profound transition in the country. But there were also elements of Iraqi history they were not familiar with because of censorship. They had so many questions of how the play came to be and how I could know this material without having lived in Iraq. I had so many questions about their lives, experiences, their studies and their dreams. It was glorious.
>
> (Najjar, personal interview, 2020)

Raffo's incredible theatrical journey was celebrated in 2018 when she was asked by the International Theatre Institute (ITI) to write a 2018 World Theatre Day message along with renowned world theater makers Ram Gopal Bajaj, Sabina Berman, Wèrê Wèrê Liking, Simon McBurney, and Maya Zbib. In her message Heather Raffo stated:

> I am an American theater artist with Iraqi heritage. My story has always been as both insider and outsider. I am both familiar and "the other." Those of us with heritage in two incommensurable cultures often find ourselves innate diplomats, adept at deep listening with the courage to express contradictory truths. It can also mean we don't fully fit anywhere—belonging remains elusive. We live and work somewhere "in between." Since I was a child I have been weighing the costs of war with the amnesia of privilege. My life's work has been to bridge Middle Eastern and U.S. culture, to balance the ancient with the modern, the communal with the pursuit of the rugged individual.
>
> (Raffo 2018)

Raffo carries the contradictory truths of being someone of American and Iraqi heritage, who lives and works in the United States telling Iraqi stories while dealing with the vestiges of wars waged on her ancestral homeland by her country of birth, and who has the unique ability to bridge the river of misunderstanding between Americans and Iraqis. "Looking back," she says, "I can see how this all contributed to how Matt and I would raise our kids as world citizens. With his work in the BBC and now the UN and my work on national and international stages, we are both so deeply committed to human narratives, to bridge building, to embracing interconnected narratives of our work" (Najjar, personal interview, 2020). Her desire to connect these disparate cultures is a noble one, but one fraught with difficulties since ours is a culture that often privileges flashy entertainment over what Raffo calls in the Afterword of this book, "works that seek to provoke a deeper spiritual, civic witnessing or reckoning from us all?" For Raffo to commit herself to writing plays that challenge dominant narratives and humanize people often considered enemies is an artistic triumph. These plays represent the voices of those who previously had no voice on American stages or have been mistranslated by American playwrights in the past. Here, Raffo is saying all those things that cannot be said and, if we are a conscientious and caring people, it is incumbent upon us to listen closely to what she is telling us.

9 Parts of Desire

Originally produced for the New York stage by Manhattan Ensemble Theater, Dave Fishelson, Artistic Director.

Originally produced by Erich Jungwirth, Voice Chair Productions; Richard Jordan, Richard Jordan Productions, Ltd.

British premiere, Traverse Theatre, Edinburgh.

London premiere, Bush Theatre, Shepherd's Bush Green, London.

An audio version of the play can be found at: https://soundcloud.com/user-348637583/sets/heather-raffos-iraq-plays-9-parts-of-desire.

*God created sexual desire in ten parts;
then he gave nine parts to women
and one to men.*

*—Ali b. Abi Talib, fourth caliph after Muhammad.
Revered as the founder of the Shi'a sect of Islam.
His shrine is in Najaf, Iraq, and is a major place of Shi'a pilgrimage.*

Characters

Mullaya
Layal
Amal
Huda
The Doctor
Iraqi Girl
Umm Ghada
The American
Nanna

Throughout the play the woman uses an abaya, a traditional black robe-like garment, to move from character to character. Some wear the abaya traditionally; others use it as a prop.

The Arabic words aa (yes) and la (no) are used throughout. Iraqi terms and lyrics to songs can be found in the Glossary.

The first sound we hear is the dawn call to prayer. In Iraq the call to prayer is heard five times a day: at dawn, midday, afternoon, sunset, and finally when the sky becomes dark and daytime is over. The call to prayer is heard five times throughout the course of this play.

The **Mullaya** *walks on stage. She has walked a great distance. She carries a large bundle on her head then empties her load of shoes into the river. Traditionally, a* **Mullaya** *is a professional mourner, hired to lead call-and-response with women mourning at funerals. She is considered very good if she can bring the women to a crying frenzy with her improvised, heartbreaking verses about the dead. Mythic, celebratory, and inviting, this* **Mullaya**'s *mourning is part of her ritual ablutions.*

Mullaya   Early in the morning
always early in the morning
I come to throw dead shoes into the river.

Without this river there would be no here
there would be no beginning
it is why I come.

Take off your slippers
take off your sandals
take off your boots
appease the hungry
so I can sleep beneath the stars without fear
of being consumed
or

the river again will flood
the river again will be damned
the river again will be diverted
today the river must eat.

When the grandson of Genghis Khan
burned all the books in Baghdad
the river ran black with ink.
What color is this river now?
It runs the color of old shoes
the color of distances
the color of soles torn and worn
this river is the color of worn soles.

This land between two rivers
I only see the one—
where is the other river
more circular and slow?
Why only this one straight and fast?
Where is the other?
And the other land?

Where is anything they said there would be?
We were promised so much
the garden of—

Let me tell you I have walked across it
Qurna, Eridu, Ur[1]
the Garden of Eden was here
its roots and its rivers
and before this garden
the chaos and the fighting
loud and angry children—
the dark sea lies beneath my country still
as it has always done
sweet and bitter water, children of Nammu.[2]
But our marshlands now are different
they've been diverted, dammed and dried.
I have walked from there to here
from the flood
to the highway of death
collecting, carrying
you can read the story
here it is, read it all here
on my sole.

My feet hurt
I have holes in my shoes
I have holes now even in my feet
there are holes everywhere
even in this story.

I don't want new shoes!
I would rather swim than walk—
bring me back the water I was created in
the water in which I woke each morning
and went to bed each night
the water in which I swam to school
and milked the buffalo
and listened to the loud voices of frogs
bring me back the marshes and the fishes
reed man, reed woman
I would rather swim than walk!
But now the river has developed an appetite for us
its current runs back

---

1. Various ancient cities and villages, all located within the current boundaries of Iraq, which are thought to be the original site of the Garden of Eden.
2. The first deity recorded in Sumerian mythology (c. 4000 BC), she is the mother of all creation who gave birth to heaven and earth. She is represented by the sea.

beneath Iraq
to where Apsu and Tiamat[3] are cradling still.
Underneath my country
there is no paradise of martyrs
only water
a great dark sea
of desire
and I will feed it
my worn soul.

Layal, *an artist, wears the abaya loosely hanging off her shoulders like a dressing gown or painting smock. She is a daredevil with a killer smile.*

Layal   Leave Iraq?

Laughing as she tries to imagine it.

Well, I could move I suppose?

My sister wants me to come to London
she has a house and an art studio there now
I could go, I have the money.

I don't know
maybe I feel guilty
all of us here
it's a shame if all the artists leave too—
who will be left to inspire the people if all the
artists and intellectuals run?
Most of them already have
my sister included.

I don't judge
I mean for most
they feel they cannot express themselves
because always it is life and death—
even I should have been dead twice before I tell you
but I'm not
death is only teasing me.

She laughs.

Maybe that's it, maybe I stay because
I feel lucky, I am charmed, what can touch me?

Besides what's to paint outside Iraq?
Maybe I am not so good artist outside Iraq?

---

3. In the Epic of Creation *Enuma Elish* (c. 2000 BC), Apsu and Tiamat are the water god and goddess who become the father and mother of all creation.

Here my work is well known
hardly anyone will paint nudes anyway
but this is us
our bodies—isn't it?
Deserted
in a void
and we are looking for something always
I think it's light.

Always I fight to keep
transparency
because once it goes muddy I can't get it back.
It's not oil, with oil you just paint over what you've done
with oil, light it's the last thing you add
but with watercolor, white
is the space you leave empty from the beginning.

I think I help people maybe
to be transcending
but secretly.
Always I paint them as me
or as a tree sometimes like I was telling you.
I don't ever want to expose exactly another woman's body
so, I paint my body
but her body, herself inside me.
So it is not me alone
it is all of us
but I am the body that takes the experience.
Your experience, yourself, I will take it
only you and I will know who it is
and the others let them say
oh Layal, again she is obsessed with her body.

I did a painting once of a woman
eaten by Saddam's son
that's how I describe it.
A beautiful young student, from University of Baghdad—
Uday he asked her out, she couldn't refuse,
he took her and beat her brutally, like is his way—
she went back to school and
her roommate saw the bruises and things and asked her "What happened?"
And she so stupid, innocent girl told her the truth.
Why she talks such things?
Iraqis they know not to open their mouth not even for the dentist.
Of course, Uday, he took her back
with his friends, they
stripped her

covered her in honey
and watched his Dobermans eat her.

See in my painting she is the branch's blossom
leaning over the barking dogs
they cannot reach
no matter how hungry they are
not unless they learn to climb her
but they are dogs, they never will.

You see, nobody knows the painting is her
but I believe somewhere she sees.

That is me, (*laughing*) my philosophy!
These stories are living inside of me
each woman I meet her, or I hear about her
and I cannot separate myself from them
I am so compassionate to them, so attached—*la, la,* it's the opposite
maybe I am separate, so separate from the women here
I am always trying to be part of them.
I feel I could have been anybody if I looked different—

Some other artists more senior than myself
would have hoped to be curator of Saddam Art Center
these jobs they are hard to come by and
it takes a lot to get them.
Always they make a rumor of me
that I got this position because I was having an affair
at that time, they said
with Saddam's cousin—
they can believe what they like
I don't care what people say.
Anyway, he's dead now of course
this cousin
a mysterious plane crash
you see?

If—
If I'd had an affair with him
how would that have made my life any easier?
Isn't everything in this country a matter of survival?
I don't care if you are with the government
or a prisoner of it.
Even loving
just the simple act of loving
can make you suffer so deeply.

So, if I am now in a position of grace, favor, rumor
so be it

I don't care
I am still trying
to be revealing something
in my trees, my nudes, my portraits of Saddam—

I fear it here
and I love it here
I cannot stop what I am here
I am obsessed by it
by these things that we all are but we are not saying.
"Either I shall die"—how does it go?
Oh my favorite, Shaharazad! (*An aching laugh*) "Either I shall die
or I shall live a ransom for all the virgin daughters of Muslims
and the cause of their deliverance from his hands to life!"

Well, I am not a person of great sacrifice
I have sacrificed in my life, sure,
but nothing like what I see around me.
Anyway, that is life. You cannot compare only be compassionate.
I try to have understanding of all sides, and I have compassion
just not enough.

I'm a good artist.

I'm an okay mother.

I'm a miserable wife.

I've loved yes, many
but
not enough.

But I am good at being naked
that's what I do, in secret.

Bright, festive, and robust, **Amal** *looks so intently at whomever she is talking to, you would swear her eyes never blinked. She asks many questions; she deeply believes there is an answer out there for her.* **Amal** *wears the abaya voluptuously about her body.*

Amal I see with my heart
not with my eyes.
I am Bedouin
I cannot tell you if a man is fat or if a man is handsome
only I can tell you if I love this man or not.
I think you see with your heart like a Bedouin.

I do, I very much feel this void
I have no peace
always I am looking for peace.
Do you know peace?

I think only mens have real peace
womans she cannot have peace
what you think?

My mother when I come home she is so happy to see me, she sing to me
she sing, "Amal my beautiful girl
Amal whose hair is black like night
Amal whose eyes are black like deep coal
Amal my daughter whose body is strong for her love"
and my voice, I have to sing to my mother, "I am home again!"
But never I think I am different
we in our village we believe our mothers.
I have *tis'ah*—nine brothers and five sisters
and nobody make me feel fat.
But I learn now I am big.
So don't you think I am fat?
La, la, I am very big
but I am diet now and my childrens too
both my childrens they are diet.
Aa, aa I have two childrens
fourteen and eight.

My husband, first husband, he was Saudi,
he is now in London
on this big road they call it
where all the big plastic surgeons are.
Aa, aa, I was there with him
I like London very much
I study there
I like to
walk with my friends in this Portobello market and—

I left him.
I was feeding my daughter, Tala, at the time
and driving my son Omar to school
I forgot some papers for Omar
so I drove back home to get them
and I saw my husband in bed with my very close friend
and really I am shock
because he is Bedouin,
but Saudi Bedouin.
And even he would say to me when I talked,
during our relations,
he'd say, "don't say these things they are dirty things".
I wanted to enjoy myself with him
but he—
and then he goes and—

So
I didn't say anything
I told a friend
go into my house
and get my passport and the children's passport
and I left
I never told him why I left.

I came back to Iraq
but I didn't like to live in our town
it's too small, I don't feel free even
always my brothers looking out for me I feel too much closed
and so I come—
not here, *la*, I—

I went to Israel first.

You see, our very close tribesman came to visit
because my father he is the sheik.
This tribesman, he is of the same Bedouin tribe as me
but born Israeli—
and always when I was a girl I thinking
oh, to marry one from my tribe
we have the same accent, same eyes, same nature, very big heart!
This tribesman he never feel the woman his enemy
he feel sorry for her and feel only to keep her happy.
And the woman she feels him very man.
We are very special together.
So, I marry him, my second marriage,
and I went to his village in Israel.

He promise me
we would move and go to Europe somewheres or Canada
but then we never move
his wife didn't want
aa, his other wife, number one, she makes him stay.
He would have taken both of us
it could have been good
but she was crazy
really she was, I think they fight a lot.
Number one, she would leave him to go to her father's house
for six months at a time and I taking care of her eight childs.
I mother one of her childs
I fed her son—oh Koran, you must know it—
if you feed for more than seven days, full feeding,
that child is like your child
and this child must never marry with your child
because now they are brother and sister in the milk

so it is *haram*, sin,
because they have your blood inside them both.
But wife, number one, she was very skinny, not well
she would go away for such a long times—
we couldn't live together like this
he is very jealousy man, very Bedouin
and I am looking for this freedom
and he says "No, we are not going to Canada."
So I care very much for him, but again
I left.

I come back to Iraq with my children
but to Baghdad to be in city.
I come here, my family don't like
they don't support me but—

I got some money.
I got some money from a friend
of my first ex-husband, this friend, his name's Sa'ad.
And we start to talk on the phone, this friend, Sa'ad,
he is in London, and me here. We talk for one year.
I talk to him honest, I am very honest person
I told him exactly I am thirty-eight, and this is how I look.
I hide nothing from him
I told him everything in my heart
everything I hope and
I felt peace.
It is beautiful to talk so much
because he
he tells me from inside himself too
very deep, very sincere
for one year.
I felt safe the first time in my life
I felt myself with this man and
I love him! (*She laughs*)

We talk and we say we will get married, third marriage, oh!
He says let us meet in Dubai
because the war it was then and if he comes back home to Iraq
they may keep him.

So I left my job, I left everything.
I telephone to his family congratulations
he telephone to my family
and we go to meet in this hotel in Dubai
we go to dinner
he says after dinner
"I am going I will call you later"

and I waiting in my hotel room so happy to see this man I love.
I telephone hims at 2 a.m. and he says, "No, not now
I am drunk"—
I say, "Let us talk I want to talk
we spent one year on the phone talking everything
finally we see each other
my heart is so full to share."
He says, "No, Amal,
no," he says, "it is over
do not talk to me anymore."
I am crying really I don't understand him say this thing
but him say,
"You are too pure for me
what you do with a man like me? I am twenty year older than you
soon I will be very olds man and you have to take care of me
you are too good, too innocent for me."
I don't understand hims say this thing because I love him,
and him says, "No,"
"No," he say,
"you are not the Amal I love."

What does this mean?
I am not the Amal he love?

How he say this?
Why can this be?

I am shamed to my family
they think he slept with me that night
we meet in Dubai
and change his mind.

I don't have peace.

Always I am asking myself what he think of me?
What he seed in me that change him?
I see now I am fat.
Now I look for the first time to dress myself more pretty
I am doing my hair this way—
but I don't see hims fat, I don't see hims old
I see hims with my heart not with my eyes
and never have I love a man this much.
Even I love him.
Even.

My ex-husband, first one,
got us passports to bring the children to London
so, they will see their father on the weekends
and have their schooling there

la, la, I think I told you this already.
But always I am thinking
what if I run into Sa'ad when I go there?
I would shake
all of me on my face
I don't know I could hide it.
I will have my freedom there
but not my peace—

Maybe freedom is the better than peace?

I have never talked this before
nobody here knows this thing about me
I keep it in my heart only
oh, I talk a lot!

I wish to be like this
I want to be like you
this is the most free moment of my life
really I mean this
oh really I love you, like a sister I love you
the most free moment of my life.
Don't leave, stay with me
oh, I need to talk everyday this way.
Is this American way?
Tell me what you think
what should I do?
I want to memorize what you say,
so I can be this way
freedom again.

She listens for an answer.

But what do think he means, I am not the Amal he love?

A whiskey drinker with fifty years as a smoker, **Huda** *is an aging Iraqi exile now living in London. It's hard to imagine her ever owning an abaya. She has a keen sense of humor.*

Huda   Well, exile in London for the intellectuals
is mostly scotch, of course politics, and poetry.
It used to be Gauloises too, but I have given up smoking
well—

Perhaps she hasn't entirely given up smoking.

Anyway, I tell you our dilemma,
some in the opposition praised America one hundred percent
they knew they were the only power
and the whole policy of the world was in their hands.
Personally, I had my doubts about American policy,

I felt they're making their own map of the Middle East,
still I preferred war to the regime
because Saddam was the worst enemy to the people than anybody else.

One summer, he beheaded seventy women for being prostitutes,
but he made them prostitutes.
Saddam's stooges, they'd kidnap a woman
just going from her car to her house,
and take her as a slave, sex slave,
or house slave when they were in their hideouts,
and when they'd finish with her
he would go to her family saying "She is a prostitute"
and he'd behead her and put her head in the street.
There was no law if you are a prostitute you are beheaded.

And where are these killers now?
Forget about peace.
We had to do something—
For three decades Saddam created monsters.
No one is born knowing how to behead, they learned torture
he took ordinary men, they were forced to watch videos
to cut off a hand, a tongue.

So I don't know, could these men have liberated themselves?

I walked for peace in Vietnam
I walked for Chile
but this war it was personal, this war was against all my beliefs
and yet I wanted it.
Because Saddam
Saddam was the greater enemy than, I mean,
imperialism.

Nauseated, **The Doctor** *washes her hands, then dries them on the abaya. Throughout she is desperate to keep her hands clean. Exhausted, she clings to the forensic.*

I'm sorry, it's probably just the smell of the sewage backing up in the ward. I feel fine, fine, let's go on, it's just, it's so hot and the smell of it makes me—

She yells offstage.

Would somebody come clean this shit up before I slip in it!

Damn it! I lost her. The baby should be dead, not her. God she had enough, she had three girls at home, but she insisted, hoping for a boy. What am I supposed to tell her husband? Here, it's your first-born son, I'm sorry he has two heads?

Look, just this month, I'll tell you, I've started counting: six babies no head, four abnormally large heads, now today another one with two heads. Such high levels of genetic damage does not occur naturally. These things you see them only in textbooks.

And the cancers, *la*, I've never seen them before in Iraq, girls of seven, eight years old with breast cancer. I told this girl, ten years old, she came in, she thought her breasts were developing but it was only on one side. It was the cancer. I told her it's okay, you can be like me, see how strong I am, I had breast cancer. She said "I want to see it," so I showed her my scar, she hugged me. She thought she was developing. But it's toddlers even with breast cancer, more than one cancer in the same patient, whole families each one suffering from cancer.

And what can stop it? I mean the children, they play at the sites even when they're fenced off, they take the bullets to school to show their classmates what they collected from America. One came in wearing a bullet around his neck, a bullet tipped in depleted uranium around his neck.

Especially here in Basra, it's in the Shatt al-Arab, so it's in all the water, it's in the food, but if it's airborne like they say – haven't you noticed something? It could be depleted uranium, or chemicals that were released from the bombings, but I can see something changed the environment – giant squash, huge tomatoes. They say the radiation in plants now is at eighty-four times the safety limit. But who can clean it? Ever? We will have this depleted uranium for, what, four thousand years? How many generations is that growing up disabled? I am afraid to see them when they're grown.

It's better maybe, death?

My husband says death is worse, *il-mawt yihrig il-glub*, death burns the heart. But I don't believe—

My husband he sits at home without his legs. He can't make money sitting at home, I can't even look at him now, he's my death sentence. I don't care, honestly, I don't care what I say. I'm a little ashamed of myself but it sickens me. We won't survive it, I won't, I'm a doctor, if I can't do anything. I trained in England, I could have gone anywhere, I came back, you know what I'm talking about, we had the best hospitals in the Middle East, everyone was coming to us, and what are we now? We're the experiment.

Look at us
look at us
wayn Allah, wayn Allah?

She is nauseated again.

No I'm fine, I'm fine
I'm pregnant.

The **Iraqi Girl** *plays with the abaya; perhaps she wraps it about her head like long luxurious hair or bundles it up to be her baby doll. However, we first catch her dancing with utter abandon in her living room to a band like 'N Sync on her new satellite TV. The electricity suddenly goes off. She yells out something like: "Momma, the electricity is out! Momma, put the generator on! Momma, my video! 'N Sync!"*

Iraqi Girl I hate my momma!
Baba, my father he said I am smart
but Momma says I am stupid.

I have not been to school
since America came
"You are stupid," she say, "you don't need to go to school."
But I think she didn't like the soldiers cames to our school
they looked like 'N Sync, mostly Justin Timberlake,
and they made all the girls to laughing really hard
and since that day she won't let me go to school
because I waved to them.

So I never leave the house.
Even though I can speaks English better than anyone.
My grandparents were scared because they don't speaks English
and soldiers came knocking on their door speaking English
it was the night
but they didn't understand
so they ran to hide under their beds
and a tank, I think it was an Abrams
they ran the Abrahams into the house
and it took down half the house.
They were eighty years old my grandparents
but they didn't speaks English.

So even we are afraid to sleeps on the roof.
In the summer I used to
put my bed on the roof under the stars
and *Baba*, my father, he used to told me
all the stories of the stars began from Babylon—
It's just down the road past Saddam City—
no,
Sadr City.

We have so much problems on TVs.
On TVs I see suicide bombings
not just for Baghdad but all over Iraq and I felt bad.
But my cousin Karem he says, "No,
no, these are not Iraqis
Iraqis don't know how to kill themselves."

I think something must be a secret
because
now we can't go anywheres without
my uncle, Ammu Abdul,
he comes here with his sons, mostly Karem and Khalid,
because we have no men.

But even they haven't taken me to the swimming pool
for two summers now.
Maybe it's dry up?
But my friend Lulu, she thinks the Americans are using it.

We don't go anywhere—
really!
Momma she doesn't even go to work anymore
she was "let off."
She never leaves the house
except to go to the market
with my uncle
and before she goes she covers her hair.
She is afraid of getting stolen by Gangs.
Now they steal women for money
or to sell them.
I try to tell Momma she won't get stolen
her hair is not that nice
they only steal people whose families have money.
But she says,
"Don't tempt your fates,
now they steal little girls to take them out of the country!"
Today I thought
maybe I should get stolens
so I could leave my country.

On TVs, on *Oprah*, I saw people
they have so many hard lives, at first we feel bad for them
but always by some miracles their things get better!
Today even they showed
Papa Saddam on TVs
and they look through his hair to make fun of him—
"Do you have lice in your hair?" That is always how we tease
in the school when we want to be the most cruel
to the poorest kids.
Do you have lice?
I don't know if he had lice
but to see it like that he looked like an old man
like a baby.
I felt sorry for him
but I didn't cry.
Momma she cried
she said, "Saddam stole my sons,
he stole my sons"—
I had three brothers who were bigger
I didn't really know them, they were martyrs,
she always says, "Saddam stole my sons."

So maybe she cries to see him on TVs
thinking now he won't give their bones back?
Because she says
"What now?"
"What now?"
"What now?"
She is very—

I am not stupid
I count bombs even
I count between the
hissing when it is high
until the sound becomes low
then two seconds . . . and it explodes!
If I hear the hissing I know it's in our neighborhood
like in a few blocks
then I hear glass breaking for four seconds
after the hit.
I can tell if it is RPGs or American,
tank or armor vehicle,
Kalashnikov or M16
and I have bullets from both
but I gave one to Karem, he made a key chain from the M16 bullet
because they are longer and he says "more elegant."
We don't have a machine gun anymore.
Everybody on our street has maybe a pistol or machine gun
in case for troubles. Now we have a pistol. But only one.
Momma taught me how to use it.

I know I am not stupid.
I found my father's notebooks upstairs
hiding under the floor
he had some math books up there and some notebooks, I took this one.
I look to it to keep my head busy
even though the maths are for people bigger than me.
And I can understand some of the maths.
But today
I read in his notebook
that "Samura," that is me, it's dated 5, October, 2002,
"Samura my beloved was at school
and they asked her
'Have you ever visited Babylon?'
And Samura, she told them, 'Of course I've been,
even at night because
my father says Saddam put his name on the bricks of Babylon
but he cannot put his name on the stars over Iraq.'
They will arrest me now for this and I am sure to die.

I should have taught her how to lie."

I remember some mens came to our house
to take my father—they said
My *baba* is so smart about the stars over Babylon
our president, he needs him.
I have not seen him since I was seven.
Momma thought when America came
he might come home
but nobody seen him
and we haven't moved.
I still want to study because if he does come home
I have to be smarter than when he left.

Actually,
I cried today too
when I saw papa Saddam on TVs
because he stole my father so
I thought he was bigger than anyone
but he didn't even fight to death.
I felt ashames, because why I am afraid from him all my life?
Momma she is right
I am stupid.

Umm Ghada *lets the abaya fall; it is a black hole. A woman of profound stillness and dispassionate pride.*

Umm Ghada   I named my daughter Ghada.
Ghada means tomorrow.
So I am Umm Ghada, Mother of Ghada.
It is a sign of joy and respect to call a parent by their *kunya*.

In Baghdad, I am famous now as Umm Ghada
because I do live here in yellow trailer
outside Amiriyya bomb shelter
since the bombing
February 13, 1991.

Yes, I was inside
with nine from my family
talking, laughing
then such a pounding, shaking
everything is fire
I couldn't find my children
I couldn't find my way out
but somehow, I did.

In the whole day later

I am searching, searching charred bodies
bodies they were fused together
the only body I did recognize
is my daughter Ghada
so, I did take her name

With so much pride.

I am Umm Ghada, Mother of Ghada.

I am hard to understand
why I survive
and my children dead.
I asked to Allah why?
Why you make me alive?
That night all people died
four hundred three people
and there's nothing we can do. They are dead.

This trailer is my witness stand
All photos on this wall—and here—are me
with emissaries from the world
who come to Amiriyya shelter to look
what really happen here
not what they read in papers
or see in the CNN.
Here is guest book they all sign,
your name will be witness too.
La, I must show it to you first. *Ta'alu.*

She enters the shelter; it is the first time we see her subtle limp.

This is Amiriyya bomb shelter.
Here they write names
in chalk over the smoked figures.
Here, on the ceiling, you can see
charred handprints and footprints
from people who lay in the top bunks.
And here a silhouette of a woman
vaporized from heat.
This huge room became an oven,
and they pressed to the walls to escape from the flames.

In the basement too
bombs burst the pipes
hot water came up to five feet
and boiled the people.

La, la, I do not want to show you there
it is too much

the walls are stuck with hairs and skin.

Come, I will take you to the roof
you can see how the hole was made.

As she walks towards the hole in the roof we hear the midday call to prayer off in the distance; she pauses briefly.

Two bombs from U.S. airplane
come to this point of the roof.
The first bomb is drilling bomb
drilled this hole
second one
come inside exactly same spot
and exploded in fires.

The U.S. said they thought this is
communication center for military.
Myself,
I think they were testing bomb
these bomb had never been use before, but it is special
two-bomb design for breaking only a bomb shelter.
It is very purpose.
It is very purpose.

Now look around this hole
wild greens they are growing
life did choose to root
here in this grave of Iraqi people.

All my family is here, Ghada is here
so, I am Umm Ghada, Mother of Tomorrow.
My full name is dead with them.

Come.
Now you sign the witness book.

Layal *picks up her paint brush.*

Layal   We have a story—
There is a restaurant with a sign
"Come in, eat all you want,
free of charge
your grandson will pay the bill."
So, a young man, a teenager,
he goes in
happy for the free meal,
he eats, and eats, and eats
when he is done eating all he wants
the waiter brings him a bill.

The young man says to the waiter,
"No, your sign says free of charge,
my grandson will pay the bill."
The waiter says, "Yes, indeed, sir,
but this—
this is your grandfather's bill."

She laughs.

My grandfather's bill!

You know my house was hit, from Bush's war, *aa, aa,*
I wasn't there, *il-hamdu lillah,*
but we lost everything, my paintings for the new exhibition
my family's things, everything.
That's why I'm living here, at my sister's house.
It was only eight houses from here—
this neighborhood they bomb, Mansur, can you believe it?
So how smart is this bomb
if it bomb a painter?

She laughs.

Maybe they think I am dangerous?

Maybe I am, I am attached like I will die if I leave.

I think you're dangerous
Americans they are not so attached this way
they feel so free, even to be alone
I am afraid to be alone
I don't want freedom—to be alone?
I don't care for it, I like protection
all I want is to feel it, love—

I am crazy for it,
I am hungry every morning like I have never eaten before,
and there is never enough to feed me
so, when I find more
I risk everything for it
oblivion even, I don't care
I submit completely.
And still I am empty
I never feel worth
because I shouldn't be so hungry
because others are not so hungry
or they can control it—but I cannot control myself
I cannot keep my mind from flesh.

I tell you, even when I fell in love
not with my husband

after I was married
really, I fell in love
it humiliated me
to finally see
how much of myself I could never be
and I hated it
not to be full
not to feel whole
it's the worst feeling this occupation
to inhabit your body but not to be able to live in it.

So, I had an affair!
I let myself love him
we were just a boy and a girl in art school
painting, drawing, very expressive
you can't imagine the freedoms
we had teachers from all over the world coming to Baghdad
I was very messy
and when my husband found out
he shot me.

I thought I was dead.

And even in the emergency room I was saying
"No, it was me
with the gun, it was me, it was an accident."
We never spoke about it
but he never stopped me from having an affair again!

I think
most women they must be so hungry
because they love with such a sacrifice
an aching
but I tell you,
when you're this way
so attached
always loving like you will die without something—
you love like an Iraqi woman! (*laughing*) Shaharazad!
Oh, Americans they have this passion to save everything
because they have such a big footprint, they feel guilty.
They are a very handsome teenager
so tall and strong
passionate, selfish, charming
but they don't think.

You have
our war now
inside you, like a burden, like an orphan
with freedom, intelligence, all opportunity and choice

yet we tether you to something so old you cannot see it—
we have you chained
to the desert
to your blood
you carry it in you, it's lifetimes
and you fight your war to unchain yourself
you come back
you feel at home here
maybe different
maybe more than in your country—
but you hate us too
because you cannot breathe
because we are not free—
you are not free, you love too much.
It's the same, all, anywhere you live
if you love like an Iraqi woman
if you love like you cannot breathe.

Huddled, **The American** *hasn't left her studio in New York City for days, she is glued to the TV.*

The American   Now they're digging through mass graves with their bare hands
and one guy on TV I saw him
he found a pack of cigarettes
and he said my brother smoked
this kind of cigarette
so, this is my brother's body
and he took the bones with him
so he could bury them
what he thought
was his brother.

I've never seen men cry like that.

I watch my dad
try not to cry
because when he's watching TV
and it's green
nighttime footage of
bombs
he can recognize the street
and the neighborhoods
where all his family
lives
still.

I watch TV
looking for

faces
of our family
so all I do is cry.
But my dad he can't
so
he ends up choking and
making himself
sick
I mean
he's lived here in the U.S.
for forty years
he plays golf
five times a week.
He's just sad
but contained
because you
can't
you just can't
watch it
on TV.
I'm on my knees usually
in the middle of my apartment
with my mom
on the phone
I'm watching
I'm holding a rosary
watching
CNN
I want to pray
but I don't have
words
so I say their names
out-loud
Sati',
Zuhayr,
Huda,
Zuhira,
Behnam,
Rabab
over and over trying
to see them
alive
because we don't know
anything
we can't
call

we can't get through on the phones
still
and
now
now people are burying their dead in their backyard
in their garden
the football field
it's everyday
a police station
my uncle Sati' lives in Baghdad next to a police station
Uncle Zuhayr lives next to the airport
Ama Huda, next to the Palestine Hotel
Ama Zuhira, in Karada, Mount Lebanon
my cousin Maysoon she used to work for the UN
but the whole face got blown off it, I'm reading on the bus—

They never forget, ever.
They carry everything with them.
I mean everything they are, they're so attached like
great-grandparents, parents, children
it lives in them, walks with them
they can't let go
of anything
they hold it all inside them.
So, when they cry
it's lifetimes
I've never seen anything like it.

Huda I can't move.

I am here in London now
this is where my husband died, in this house
and I didn't change a thing from that time I kept the house the same,
his picture, everything.

I was invited to go back.
So many people I was working with have returned but—

I have moved five times in my life, always fleeing
Baghdad, Lebanon, Istanbul, Baghdad again, anyway.
America offered me lots of money to go back
but I don't believe in this, some Iraqis
they are just selling themselves.

I said let the young ones living there have a chance with the policies.
But they are shell shocked, all these girls
they're going backwards
they abandon their education and now,
now they are wearing the veil. Even the feminists are wearing the veil.

Their grandmothers are more liberated than them.

No. I'm not being fair.
There's a whole generation today,
they want to think for themselves, without Iran, without America,
they grew up never knowing Saddam.
Maybe what they face now is worse than Saddam?

Everywhere there is civil war. It's tearing me—
Ya'ni, we had fine interrelations,
my family married with the Shi'a, my husband was a Kurd
there was no segregation sort of thing. These people
they have been living together in this area for thousands of years.
We never knew if our neighbor was Sunni or Shi'a—it was offensive to ask.
Now in London even, people demand to know what I am.
I don't recognize my country.

We missed our moment, during the first Gulf War
Iraqis were ready, the whole country was united
the people made this big rebellion—
sixteen of the eighteen provinces fell
and they were sure America would help them, the CIA offered—
then America turned its back. They made a no-fly zone
but when they saw Saddam going with his helicopters
to execute his own people
they allowed him to fly. It was a blood bath
Saddam killed tens of thousands, trucks full,
and buried them just mass graves.
If we had helped the people get rid of him then
we would not now have—

No, the mistake is not the war
we had to do it
the mistake was supporting Saddam all his life.

When America imposed this thirteen years' suffering—
what do you call it? *Hisar*? Embargo?
It made Saddam stronger
and the country more backwards and religious,
and funny enough Saddam he was never religious,
but when the middle class
were selling their books on the street in order to eat
they felt the whole world had abandoned them.
And this gutting of the middle class, of what kept the country together, the region,
cannot now be changed back.
We just gave the fundamentalists their legitimacy.
And now they're controlling the country. So, Iran too is controlling
and ISIS, well—

it started in Iraq but where will it end?

I don't know if I believe anymore in revolution, *ya'ni*
to really change the values?
Development must grow carefully, gradually, not suddenly
it has to grow more deep rooted.
Even though I can say
we all can say
congratulations
the regime is gone.
Saddam is gone.

Impossibly old and shrewd, **Nanna** *has seen it all. She sells anything she can on the street corner. She wears the abaya traditionally over her head so only her face and hands remain showing. The third call to prayer sounds in the distance.*

Nanna Hallo hallo
you like to buy?
These things very nice
very old
from good family.
We have old
no
not that old.
Not ancient.

Shhh
not loud in ENGLISH—
you want
my head on
the side of the road?

I have for you
but—
shhh.

You
should
fear
before there was
one,
now
everyone
is Saddam,
looking
what you are
your accent
your name—
What you sell?

Where you get it?
From who?
What neighborhood?
What your first name?
You must be Shi'a
You must be Sunni
Middle class?

She makes a motion indicating having her throat slit.

I tell you
everything I have
here's
stolen.
My name
my accent—
my own mother
wouldn't recognize me.

She laughs.

I'm not thief!
Chal chal alayya!
It's freedom to have!

Hallo hallo
you like to buy?
Very nice
very old, from good family—

I have too much existence
I have lived through twenty-three revolutions
my life has been spared
if my life has been spared
to whom do I owe my debt?
I have so much to repay.
To whom do I owe my debt?

I give you
old
history old
from the beginning,
shhh,
I saw from the beginning, the looting
peoples
bringing petrol,
and
burning
all

National Archives,
Qur'anic Library
all—
I saw a map
they knew what to take
they were told what to take
I followed
I took
and nobody stopped me
then they burned them gone.
Our history is finished.
Sunni, Shi'a, Kurd,
Christian even, Jew—
if they take what we share
it is easier
to finish.

When I was young in the school
they had us to draw
our family tree—
my mother had a new dress
it's with ruffle and flowers
that I loved
and she wear it in the house
I think every day for many weeks.
So, I draw my mother like a big flower
with ruffles.
My teacher say, no
it is wrong before Allah
drawing her hair and her body showing
I am disrespecting.
So, I look to the other children and
they drawing only the fathers and grandfathers
because of the name line.

So, I just erased her, my mother,
it was only pencil.

The American   Here
there's space
we throw our arms wide
amber alerts and
seven men get trapped underground
and we stop everything
we fly in engineers
to save
everything
we make a movie

we go on *Oprah*, we talk about it
like we are moving on
or maybe
we can't move on
but just one trauma we say
Okay
this can change you
possibly
your psychology, for the rest of your life
Okay.
But there's no one saying—

when their parents get
blown apart
in front of their eyes
or their sons
are kidnapped
trying to go to work
or hacked
to death
and there's a head in my *ammu*'s front yard—
or they survive
everything
over and over and over again for as many years as I've been alive
my cousins
who are, who could have been
the exact same as me
told me they wouldn't
get married
because if they
someday
saw a chance
to get out
they had to take it
and not look back.
They never stop looking back.
The three that escaped
they had to watch it on TV
the second war
they said maybe it's worse seeing it on TV
sick, they can't protect the family.
But my dad said
maybe it's better
for the future
but if we lose
just one
one

it won't be
worth it.

Behnam
Rabab
Ammar
Bashar
Nassar
Luma

I should get out
get something to
eat.
I'm fat.
I should just go to the gym and run.
God I'm so stressed out
maybe
I should take a yoga class instead?

Anyway, I can watch it at the gym
people work out
to the war
on twenty-three channels.
They drink beer at the bar to the war.
I hear everything people say.
I can't stop
I wake up and fall asleep with the TV on
holding a rosary
watching—
I know
I should just
turn it off
but I won't
I hate it when people say
I don't watch it
anymore
it depresses me
yeah
it depresses me
I can't
breathe—

I'm sick
my stomach
I can't get out of my—
it's a beautiful warm day
and I'm a cave.
I can't walk down the street

and see people smiling
dragging bodies through the street
for the rest of my life
Iraqis are animals cheering, dragging bodies through the street.
But my family can't even leave their house
and I can't call
still
and we're
smiling
pointing
at
a man
naked
with a sand bag on his head
raped
with a chemical light, told to masturbate.
I cannot carry it
and they're
thumbs up
smiling
don't tell me
they didn't know
their job
not with smiling
every photo
they were
smiling.

How can I ever
go home again
and sit
in my *amma*'s kitchen
and say
I'm sorry
I'm sorry
I'm—
we just keep going
subway
rush rush
Christmas shopping
and
the war, it's all so heartbreaking don't you think?
I don't even know
hundreds of thousands?
How many Iraqis?
And

a woman actually turned to me
and said that
she said
"The war it's all so heartbreaking."
She was getting a pedicure.
I was getting a fucking pedicure.
I walk
I can't walk
down
the street
I want
New York to stop.
Why don't we count the number of Iraqi dead?

Why?

Layal Why are you here?

Don't look at me like that
always this pressure on me
I can't bear it—your look.

You tell me about freedom, about choice and possibilities,
then you look at me like a whore for choosing to paint myself naked
and you look at me like a whore for choosing to paint portraits of Saddam
and now you look at me like a whore for thinking, just thinking
to do this mosaic for the floor of the Rashid Hotel?
But what are you creating with your freedom? I am more free than you.

You beg me to leave
to get out while I can, I am getting too involved
insisting I get out for my safety.

Why? What is safe? There is no safe.

I wish I were afraid
I am beyond afraid—
I am just running, running
straight into it
always like this I am running
since the day my husband shot me
because I should have been dead
but I wasn't—
So what am I?
Why am I alive?
To be made love to? Passed around from one man to another?
His cousin, his brother, the ministers of—

If I am not afraid then there is no feeling.

Your eyes say to me that I am a whore
their eyes say I am the most beautiful woman in Baghdad
I am their fountain
I have been raped and raped and raped and raped
they see me, they recognize me for what I am
that is freedom
they will never kill me—

Huda —we just woke up
we heard a shot and gunfire and things and
we thought it would pass and something would happen
nothing.
We gathered all the friends, in the street you know
to see what's going to happen
and we never went back to our house
this was the coup, 1963, it was a Friday.
They came with their Kalashnikovs and their boots and so on
going house by house arresting people.
I was held, eh, two and a half months,
my husband four and a half months,
we were pro-Abd al-Karim Qasim, we were the leftist.
One hundred eighty thousand people
were just arrested from Baghdad and all the elite you know,
the artists and architects, everybody, intellectuals—
we were Communist then but not violent, the Ba'thist only took us
because we disagreed.

The prison status was terrible
we stayed lying on the floor
only lying like sardines.
I remember one woman she got her period.
You know what they do when a woman gets her period?
They hang her upside down naked
so, her blood runs, for her whole cycle like that, upside down.
Anyway. That was that.

But their way, I promise you, their way
was to torture the people close to you
that is how they'd do it.
One woman I was with
they brought her baby, three-month-old baby, outside the cell
they put this woman's baby in a bag with starving cats
they tape-recorded the sound of this and of her rape
and they played it
for her husband in his cell.
That is how they do it.

So how these people could have liberated themselves?

Anyway, nightmare.

When we got out of jail we made passports, fake passports,
and we fled across the desert with our wet clothes on our back.
I did washing
but we didn't wait to dry them.

She laughs and hacks.

Myself too, it takes a lifetime to be liberated.

Okay, are you hungry? I'm having another whiskey.

She pours herself another drink.

You think the people don't want liberation? Still.
Everyday they risk more than we can conceive
just to go to work
to school
to live there is a protest.

How many Iraqis have died trying to get their country back?
Protect them, empower them.
Otherwise to live like this it is not liberation it is masochism.

A loud bombing raid; everything is shaking. **Layal** *screams into the phone.*

Layal   When is this going to stop?

I don't care what time it is.
Why don't you do something about it?
I hear the sounds, something, like it's in my house
and I can't make it through another one.

La, targets!
How they blow up a house in this neighborhood?
This is a rich neighborhood
and they say it is an accident?
No, it is on purpose or stupidity!
How they do it?
Why my house?
I feel like an animal every time I hear that sound.
I am tired, I want my house back—

No, I am sorry.

No, eh—
of course, it's late, your wife, she's next to you
I'm just, I am angry and I don't know where to be in this.

No, my husband he sleeps upstairs
he can sleep through anything.

Don't ask me now again.
I told you I don't know how to do mosaic.
I am a painter, why he wants me?
I don't know how.

La, don't tell him I don't want to do it, just tell him
I am not so good at it
I have no knowledge for mosaic.
Okay, I think about it
I'm just angry now and
why can't you do something?

Oh
not tonight I mean—

No of course, I think of you
I'm
I'll come tomorrow
Okay
at your office
Okay.
Fine. Fine. Fine.

She hangs up the phone.

Shahryar!

I said yes to the mosaic.

A man's voice cuts in on a telephone answering machine. His voice is loud and urgent. It is **The American**'s *uncle calling her from Baghdad.*

First Uncle Phone Call
Hallo Hallo Hallo
I am your uncle calling from Baghdad.
We have tried to phone you since Tuesday.
We are very sorry—

The American   —it's just his beautiful broken English
he calls me his heart's
daughter
my uncle Behnam
trying
to reach me
for three days
they saw the dust and the papers blowing
everything they saw New York on TV.
He called to say
he was sorry
can you believe that?

Sorry for my great city
hopes this never happens again—
all the family
worried sick about me.
And
my family in Michigan
they all called my parents in Michigan to see if I was okay
I know they love me but
they didn't call me personally
and my Iraqi family are calling from halfway around the world
calling New York
they didn't stop until
they heard my voice.

Our last conversation
was before the bombs started in Baghdad
I finally got through to my aunt
and I'm screaming into the phone
"I'm calling from New York, I'm calling from"—

Second Uncle Phone Call

Again on voice-over.

Hallo Hallo Hallo
we have tried to phone you since Tuesday
we are very sorry to hear this terrible things happen.
Our family worry about you—

Layal *rushes to answer the phone.*

Layal
Hallo! Hallo! Sabah? *Habibti*! My daughter!
Shlonich?
Aa, aa, fine, fine we are okay, okay,
how are you?

Aa, aa, I know our phones they don't work for sure. (*She laughs.*)

I'm calling for three week but we couldn't get through
oh *Habibti*, my daughter, I kiss you, I hold you oh, I miss you
I miss you, *Habibti*
I miss you—

La—don't come home
not this summer.
Stay
take some summer classes or,
why not go to your aunt's house in London? *Aa*?

La, la—

It's, getting sort of
well it's getting very hot already and, eh
the air condition is broken
we are old fashioned now even me, who can believe it?

Sabah, it is too hot for you to come home!

The line is cut off.

Sabah? Hallo?
Hallo?
Sabah?
Sabah?

Third Uncle Phone Call

Again on voice-over.

Hallo Hallo
We are very sorry to hear this terrible things happen.
Our family worry about you.
We hope you are always well
and wish you all the happiness.
Again, we are deeply, deeply sorry
and hope this will never happen again.
We love you very much.
All the family does love you.
We are waiting for you to visit us.
You must come and visit us.
It is very hard for us to come to you
but you must come here
and visit us.
And you must bring your father
and you must bring your mother
and you must bring your brother.
We are waiting for you
we miss you very much, all the family,
your uncles and aunts with their children
and we love you
we are waiting for you.

The American   "I'm calling from New York!" I'm screaming into the phone,
our last call before the bombs started and
my Amma Ramza finally picks up the phone
the first thing she says to me
clear as English is
"Go to church and pray"
her only other English is "I love you"
I love you
Habibti, Habibti

I love you
I love you
I love you
I love you
I love you
I love you
I love you
I love you
I love you
Behnam
Rabab
Ammar
Bashar
Nassar
Luma
Fadhila
Mazin
Zena
Nadia
Zuhayr
Mufida
Karem
Rashid
Muther
Zuhira
Jaber
Geanne
Siba
Reem
Rand
Ramza
Zaki
Aubai
Rawah
Raid
Mary
Jacob
Muna
Huda
Nabil
Maryam
Salma
Adnan
Fadiya
Layth
Maysoon

Yousif
Zayd
Sa'ad
Farah
Ayad
Zyad
Nadia
Majd
Marwan
Salaam
Basil
Sati'
Aamira
Melad
Masarra
I love you
I love you
I love you
I love you
I love you
I love you
I love you
I love you
I love you
I love you
I love you
I love you
I love you
I love you
I love you
I love you
I love you
I love you
I love you
I love you
I love you I love you
on and on like that
five minutes, ten minutes
until they cut the phones off.

And—

Layal   I will never leave
not for freedom you do not even have
call me what you like, look at me how you will
I tell you
so many women have done the same as me

everywhere they have to do the same.
If I did the same in your England or America
wouldn't they call me a whore there too?
Your Western culture, sister, will not free me from being called a whore
not my sex
women are not free
go home
you are cold, you are a cave
go back to your safety.

I will do whatever he asks of me.
But this
I do this for me, this is for me—

Suddenly genuinely amused.

I will make the mosaic of Bush's face
on the floor of the Rashid Hotel
and I will write in English for all the world to read
"Bush is Criminal."
Why not? What's the worst?
Everyone walking into the hotel
will walk across his face.
And I will walk across his face.

She begins to upend her art studio. She smashes pottery and anything she can find as she looks to make pieces for the mosaic.

Everyday I risk more
than you can conceive
without my legs
buried in the backyard
they're making their own map of
me anyway—sure after every
bomb
first bomb drilling bomb
all I want is to feel it—love
we were just a boy and a girl
bodies were fused together—
second bomb come inside exactly same spot
here—he made them prostitutes
eight houses from here
don't come home
I am not the Layal he loved
third bomb—boil the people
I don't want freedom
Mullaya why are you here?
so old you cannot see it

yaboo, yaboo
I'm fine, I'm fine, I'm   (**Layal** *begins to beat her face and chest.*)
la ilaha illa Allah   (*The fourth call to prayer is heard.*)
la ilaha illa Allah
la ilaha illa Allah

I'm dead.

*The **Mullaya** finds herself in the remains of **Layal**'s life; she picks up and holds the pieces of her fractured language. However, what was for **Layal** explosive and destructive is for the **Mullaya** a build towards a whole.*

Mullaya   A silhouette of a woman
vaporized from heat.
In a void
deserted
fighting to keep transparency.
My body, but her body
herself, inside me.
Why do you look at us as we have two hearts?
We have only one heart.
You know us better
and all what is left of us
Baba oh *Baba*
I have too much existence.
I have lived through seven thousand revolutions!

To the well one day you'll return
thirsty, assured it will be there
but you'll not find—spring, nor river
so beware of throwing a stone
into the well.
Paint with real restraint
always fight to keep transparency
because once you go past
between the shore and the river
it goes muddy, it's muddy forever.
The marshes are witness
if you drink water out of the well
it's the space you leave it empty from the beginning.

Look
around this whole.
I'm afraid to see them
when they're grown
wild greens they are growing
life did choose to root
here in this grave.
All my family is here

same accent
same eyes
same nature
very big heart
we couldn't live together like this?
Always it is life and death
and life and death—

She steps into the river, raising water to her face. As she continues, she becomes fully immersed.

Carry it with you
so when they cry
so old you cannot see it.
Try to reach me
for three days
hear my voice
upside-down
broken English
collecting
carrying
house by house.
I can't move
I can't breathe
I cannot choose to leave
throw our arms wide
sing to my mother
I am home again.
Oblivion even
I don't care
I submit completely!

Late in the evening
always late in the evening
I come to collect worn soles from the river
because
I love you
I love you
I love you
I love you.
I fear it here
and I love it here
I cannot stop what I am here.
Either I shall die
or I shall live a ransom for all the daughters
of Savagery.
She called it Savagery
when you love like you cannot breathe.

We hear the fifth and final call to prayer. Darkness; it is the end of the day's cycle.
Nanna *hoards what is left of the props, indeed everything she now owns, desperate to make a sale.*

Nanna   Hallo, hallo.
Hallo.
You like to buy?
These things very nice, very old,
from good family
we have books
carpet
shoes.

Seeing an opportunity, **Nanna** *grabs* **Layal**'s *painting.*

Hallo, hallo.
You like this painting?

It is very worth
she call it Savagery
famous artist
her name
Layal—

You recognize? *Aa*,
I was her neighbor
I knew her good
bomb fell her house
la, la, again, another bomb, her sister house,
she dead
her husband dead
her daughter blind.
Aa, aa, very sad—
so it is more worth
more worth!

She is martyr, all of us
all, the president he used to love her, he praise her
he put her painting in
Baghdad Museum of Art.
It was full only his portrait.
Room and room of him.
And I did saw it
he put her body, her trees
next to his face.
You must buy, buy
you must buy.

I tell you

this her last painting alive
all the rest
they are burned dead in the museum.
I run
I took it.
Our history is finish
so, it is more worth
more worth.

I give you secret
some trees are womans
this one, little one, is me
I let her paint me
aa, she see me
shhh
don't say
my husband he thinks it's just a tree.

I have to sell it
I have to eat
two dollar?

Nanna's *outstretched hand demands more than it asks.*

Two dollar?

Blackout

Fallujah

Libretto by Heather Raffo

Fallujah was originally commissioned by City Opera Vancouver through the initiative of Charles Annenberg Weingarten. It received its world premiere at Long Beach Opera in March 2016 and its New York premiere at New York City Opera in November 2016. The composer was Tobin Stokes and the story consultant Christian Ellis.

Characters

Philip *USMC, Lance Corporal Houston. African American. His time in the marines began in Fallujah, Iraq in 2004. In this opera we see him on suicide watch during a rare moment his emotions have had space to fully surface. This is his fourth suicide attempt since returning home from war.*

Rocks *USMC, Private Richards. Any race. Physically the strongest of all the marines. The biggest heart.*

Lalo *USMC, Senior Lance Corporal Lopez. Latinx. Senior in this group of marines. Ever the diplomat.*

Corpsman *HM3 Harris. Any race. Often nicknamed "Doc." A young man in the navy who serves as a medic with the marines. When needed, he even fights alongside the marines. He is a brother in battle to Philip, not a medical doctor.*

Taylor *USMC Lance Corporal. African American. A young dad and a trickster. Philip's best friend.*

Wissam *An Iraqi boy from Fallujah. Older than his years.*

Shatha *Wissam's Iraqi mother. Practical and strong in the face of war.*

Colleen *Philip's adopted mother. Any race. Careful with emotion, steadfast, vigilant.*

Kassim *An Iraqi man from Fallujah who fights in the Iraqi resistance. A nationalist not fundamentalist.*

The set is sparse. It is simultaneously a room that hints at a veterans hospital or a clinic in Fallujah. There are multiple levels. From the top level one can see a great distance. The top level doubles as the rooftop of a house in Fallujah. A single military cot sits alone, like an isolated island on the ground level. There is one door to the ground-level room. With lights the stage can have the warmth of a beautiful Iraqi evening, or the shadows of a dark street before a battle. The cast can easily enter and exit into shadow. They can remain on stage but not always visible to our main character, **Philip***, a young marine.*

Scene One

Philip *sits on the edge of his cot facing the open door. He listens to music on his earphones but is alert and vigilant. As a marine, he never sits with his back to the door.*

It is the required seventy-two hours holding at a veterans hospital following a suicide attempt. As per military hospital rules, the door must be left open during these seventy-two hours so he can be watched.

The **Corpsman** *walks into* **Philip***'s room.* **Philip** *takes off his belt and shoelaces and empties his pockets. The* **Corpsman** *then checks under the mattress and is about to leave the room. He comes back to collect* **Philip***'s earphones. When the* **Corpsman** *confiscates the earphones the raging sound in* **Philip***'s head begins to fill the theater.*

Colleen*,* **Philip***'s mother, stands urgently. She is two stage levels above. She listens intently for a sign of* **Philip***'s condition.*

Philip *crosses to close the door.*

Colleen Philip? Philip?
Open the door!
you've got to open the door!

Philip Only music can keep me
keep me in
keep me—

Music builds.
The cast reveal themselves in the shadows around **Philip***.*

Rocks Nobody's gonna know who he is.

Corpsman His face is gone.

Taylor Take your boot off his head.

Lalo He's playing possum.

Colleen We've been here before.

Kassim The body blown back,
to where we picked it from the dirt.

Taylor Did she cry when you almost died?

Shatha Then she's your mother.

Colleen Philip, stop!
Whatever you're doing, stop it!

Philip Can't feel
what's wrong
can't heal
what's gone.
Wanna hurt
but nothing hurts.
Too dangerous to be alive
dangerous to be outside
where nothing hurts—
find hurt
to stop me from going numb.

Used to feel
Responsibility.
Can't see
can't care
you, my only family.
I'll disappoint
you hurt
feel hurt—
Why can't I stop feeling numb?

Colleen Philip I can't hear you. I need to hear you—

Philip You adopted me into more
than I was ready for.
Never had anything—
born in a basement
born to a whore.
I was given to you
because it wasn't safe for me.

That should hurt
make me hurt.
Make me more
more than numb.

You asked me to choose
what kind of life mine would be
new start, new mom
our territory—

Colleen Put your hands down, whatever you're doing,
listen, listen to me
hands down.

I stopped you before.
I gave you something to fight for.
Philip. Just open the door.
You've got to open the door.

Philip Does it matter I'm a man
a marine—
made something of myself
made you proud, made you sure
war made something else out of me.

Colleen Philip, find something to write with
a pen, marker,
write my name
on your skin.

An Iraqi boy steps out from the shadows.

Wissam My name's Wissam.

Wissam. I'll write it for you,

Wissam.

He writes his name in Arabic on the inside of **Philip***'s arm.*

Wissam And your name?

Colleen Write "Mom"
on your wrist, your neck, your head.

Rocks Nobody's gonna know who he is.

Corpsman His face is gone.

Lalo He's playing possum.

Philip This place is gonna be ash it's
gonna eat through your skin
only our clothes will be left.

Colleen Look at my name on your skin
if you hurt yourself, I'm there with you.

Philip I've been awake
for months
smelling burnt flesh.
The eyes of a mother
a boy
in my bare hands

a boy
making a monster of me.

Wanna be done
back alive
put me back
back inside.
Let me hurt
have to hurt
to stop me from
going numb.

The door to **Philip***'s room slams shut.*

Colleen   Philip! I can't lose another son.

Scene Two

Startled by the sound, **Philip** *and* **Taylor** *jump to the upper level. This is Fallujah, where the marines have taken over a clinic as an observation point. The other men stationed about the multi-story clinic become alert at the sound of the loud noise.*

Philip   They said four bodies and two of them were—

Lalo   Were what?

Philip   Corpses in black were hung from "Brooklyn Bridge."

Taylor   Women?

Philip   No, Blackwater.
Burnt. Like charcoal.
Dragged through the street
then hung off a bridge.

Rocks   This place makes me hate more every day.

Philip   Wonder what they got out of them?

Taylor   There's nothing left of them.
They're in pieces.

Lalo   The whole city will be punished
for those stupid few.

An Iraqi boy is seen on the upper level. **Wissam** *tries to stand but is stumbling.*

Philip   Haji boy!
Stop.
Qif qif!

Lalo   Is he armed?

Taylor   He might be wounded—

Lalo   He might be loaded.

Taylor   He's a boy.

Rocks   He's an animal.

Philip   They're all animals.
I've seen that boy before
holding a corpse.

He's got something
he's cupping his hands.

What's he got in his hands?
His hands!

Wissam *holds out his hands gently.*

Philip   I said stop—you son of a bitch—

Colleen *suddenly stands.*

Colleen   Stop!
Philip, I know you.
I can hear you breathing.

Scene Three

The navy **Corpsman** *opens the door, light streams in. Present day, psych ward recovery room of VA hospital. The marines subtly shift positions. Perhaps they never leave the stage, they never leave* **Philip**.

Corpsman   Your mother's outside waiting to see you.

Philip *doesn't take his eyes off* **Wissam**.

Philip   How close?

Corpsman   Just talk to her, you don't have to go home with her.

Philip   How close? Define my kill zone.

Corpsman   You don't have one anymore, Houston.

Philip   Once you have one,
you have to have one.

Corpsman   In here you don't.
And VA rules, you gotta keep the door open.

Philip   Do you know how tired I am
keeping myself on a leash?

And my mom wants to walk in here
and throw her arms around me?

I did my job
we both did—
You sew people up,
you can still sew people up.

Corpsman   Listen, Houston
You came back in one piece—

You're only in here for seventy-two hours.
After that they don't care what you do
as long as you don't try to hurt yourself again.

Have you slept at all?

Philip   I never sleep.

Corpsman   Well you should try.
Use it as a time to get some peace.

Philip   I tried that.

Corpsman   You half tried.
Look—you called me.
I sew people up?
I won't deal with the death of one more buddy who made it back alive
it's backwards. If you wanted to die
I'd have killed you over there.

An Iraqi woman enters **Philip's** *mind. As* **Shatha** *attempts to make her way home, she brushes past* **Philip** *wearing her traditional long, black abaya. She walks dangerously close. Everything in Fallujah feels dangerously close.*

Scene Four

Philip *jumps to readiness offering the woman a trained greeting; hand on heart, eyes down.* **Taylor** *sensing* **Philip** *is about to get hazed, steps in. This is daily life in Fallujah, part humor, part boredom, part threat.*

Taylor   Excuse me, miss, I am in real need of a blow job
think of it as a simple but meaningful service
to your cunt-ry.

Lalo (*to* **Philip**)   Houston! You idiot!
I trained you on that greeting
but the way you do it
you look like you're
bowing to the Queen of England.

Get some balls.
You look like Gandhi gone gay.

Taylor We gotta respect their women—
Houston is full of respect.

Lalo (*still to* **Philip**) Houston, never
let a woman pass that close to you.
They can hide all manner of shit under that robe.

Taylor That is precisely why I asked to see her private—

Lalo Taylor, you're a pain in the ass
watch your language with the ladies.

Taylor I was getting important intel
on if she spoke English or not.

Rocks Did she speak English?

Philip How the hell would you know?

Taylor She smiled in English.

Lalo You're too stupid to live.

Taylor How do you save a black man from drowning, Corporal?
You take your boot off his head.

Beat.

I'm forgetting how to fight.

Rocks It takes ten minutes to get permission to kill a haji holding an RPG.

Taylor Forget it, Houston, she's somebody's mother,
she wasn't hiding anything.

Why all the training if we can't use our heads?

Lalo When was the last time you used your head?

Philip You don't have a head.

Taylor You're a real killer, Houston.

My mother may have dropped me on my head at birth, but I turned out just fine.
Better than what your mother did to you, pretty boy.

Better than that Iraqi woman giving birth
The doctor finally got the baby out
And SLAM, he threw it against the wall
Picked it up, looked at it again, then
SLAM he threw it against the other wall—

Philip You can't kill what's dead.

Rocks   You're sick—

Philip   Shit,
Haji kid
at my three.

Philip *sees* **Wissam**.

Lalo   What's he doing?

Philip   On the rooftop
with a weapon.

Taylor   How many meters?

Lalo   What kind of weapon?

Philip   Looking like an RPK
twenty meters out.

Wissam *extremely anxious, fiddles with a gun.*

Rocks   I'll green com.

Philip   It's an AK47.

Lalo   Is he aiming?

Philip   No.

Lalo   Don't bother.

Philip   He has a goddamn rifle.

Lalo   He is not coming toward you.
He is not aiming.
Hold fire.

Rocks   What does it take?

Taylor   He's a kid, man.

Philip   Roger. Kid.

Lalo   Does he see us?

Philip   He looks stupid.

Taylor   He looks like he never held a gun before.

Lalo   Most of them haven't.

Rocks   No, they shoot with their eyes closed
it's a religion thing.

Taylor   They don't kill on Friday?

Lalo   They take the soul if they see the kill
so they shoot with their eyes closed.

Taylor   No shit you take the soul—it's called killing.

Philip   He's putting it down.

Taylor   He's scared.

Philip   He's running off.

Lalo   He basically doesn't know
what the hell he's doing.

Philip   And now we have to wait for him to come back
when he does.

Rocks   Great, let him kill us later.
I love this hearts and minds shit,
one in the mind, two in the heart.

Taylor   He's just a boy.

Rocks   With a rifle.

Corpsman   There is no such thing as an innocent kid with an AK47.

Philip   They're innocent
too innocent.

Problem is they don't have anything to lose.

Beat. The men go back to boredom.

Philip   You heard from your family yet, Taylor?
Your son born yet?

Taylor   Still waiting to hear.

Corpsman   What are you looking at then? You been staring inside your helmet all day thought you had a picture of your son.

Taylor   No, it's a new pic of my daughter.
She turns one today.

Lalo   One? And another baby on the way?
God you knocked your wife up fast.

Philip   Let's see your kid.

Taylor   What is one?

It's laughing with her head thrown back
kissing with her cheek
crawling in her sleep.

I can see in one photo
more than a letter can tell.
Her eyes ask
where I am
and who I am
and who I'm gonna be
when I get home.

Her momma says she sees everything
and wants it for herself
your dinner, your beer, your boots.

Is she gonna see this war written on me?
Is she gonna feel it in my touch?
Is she gonna know me?
Know to call me Dad?

Her eyes talk to me all the time
since the hour she was born
her whole hand tight around my finger
her eyes fixed to mine
asking if I'm gonna be there
to feed her
when she's hungry.

I don't know if she needs this war.
I don't know if she is what I do it for.
I only know I have so much
I have too much to—

The door slams shut, a loud single crack.

Lalo   Sniper!

Rocks   Holy fuck!

Lalo   Incoming!

Corpsman   Did it impact?

Rocks   It's the kid
we should've eliminated him.

Lalo   Can't be a local
it's too accurate.

Corpsman   Where's the round?

Rocks   We're lying here like dinner!

Philip   His brains
his brains are in my mouth!

The marines now see **Taylor** *has been shot.* **Kassim** *watches in the shadows.*

All   Corpsman!
Corpsman up!

Lalo (*to* **Corpsman**)   No, keep back, there is nothing left—
(*To marines.*) Get down! Get covered!

Philip   I'm covered in him
he's all over me.

Corpsman   Pick him up!
All of him! Get ALL of him!

The men pull **Taylor** *off* **Philip**. *They drag the body.*

Corpsman   Shit.
Get the rest of his head.
Bag it.

Rocks   What you gonna do with it?

Philip   You're sending it home?

Corpsman   You want me to leave your brains in Fallujah?

Rocks   His face is gone
nobody's gonna know who he is.

Lalo   —or know to call him dad.

They drag the body to the corner and crowd together with their backs against the closed door. The men huddle, breathing, waiting for a moment of safety. One of them eventually runs out to check the observation point before signaling it's clear.

Scene Five

The marines stand one by one in a battalion formation when called. They only have each other; they have to account for their own.

Lalo   HP3 Harris.

Corpsman   Here.

Corpsman   Senior Lance Corporal Lopez.

Lalo   Here.

Lalo   Private Richards.

Rocks   Here.

Rocks   Lance Corporal Houston.

Philip   Here.

Philip Lance Corporal Taylor.

Silence.

Rocks Lance Corporal Joseph Taylor.

A longer silence.

Lalo Lance Corporal Joseph C. Taylor.

A longer silence still.

Taylor *stands and puts his kevlar/helmet on* **Philip***'s cot and exits Fallujah. He crosses to a distant part of the stage where he watches over his buddies. He can see* **Kassim** *now, the man who shot him. The other men disperse unaware.*

Scene Six

Philip *crosses to his cot and picks up* **Taylor***'s helmet. He looks inside at the photo of* **Taylor***'s daughter. The other men stay in position. It is a subtle shift back to the VA hospital, all the men in a visceral and personal memory of* **Taylor***'s death.*

Philip What is one?
His eyes talk to me all the time
since the hour he was killed
his whole hand tight around my shoulder
his eyes fixed to mine
asking if I'm gonna be there
to save him
when he's dying.

I don't know if I need this war
I don't know if he is what I do it for.

Colleen Philip?

Rocks I carried his head for days
tattooed his name on my hand.
But my tattoo got blown in two.
You'd think that would be the end of it
but I still carry him, everywhere.

Colleen Philip?

Lalo Can't rest
can't dim the lights
left a piece of myself there
can't be anywhere but there.

Philip He was so much more than me.

Colleen I've found you before

I'll give you something to fight for.

Philip So much to give, so much to live for.

Colleen I did not replace the son I lost with you.

Philip He was so much more than me.
Problem is,
I don't have anything to lose.

Colleen I know what you're about to do
I'm here—
I won't—
I can't stop you.

Adopting you was something true
you were eight years old
that's old enough, you chose me too.
I made you my son
but you made a mother of me.

Philip? Philip.
I'm here.
I'm here.
Can you hear me breathing?

Scene Seven

The **Corpsman** *opens the door to* **Philip**'s *room at the VA hospital.*

Corpsman It's late—gonna see your mom before lights out?

Philip I can still taste his brains in my mouth.

Corpsman Philip, your mom's been sitting outside
going on nine hours now,
she just wants to see you
let her in, you'll both sleep better.

Philip She's not my mother.

Corpsman Last name Houston—
who else would she be?

Rocks At least she doesn't have to change your pants.

Lalo She's almost as pretty as you.

Philip I'm adopted.

Lalo We all are. Nobody comes back to the same family.

Taylor *stands.* **Philip** *feels his presence.*

Taylor Did she raise and feed you?
Did she write you letters when you were over there?
Did she cry when you almost died?

Then she's your mother.

Scene Eight

A woman in a long black abaya again brushes closely past **Philip** *at his cot. She walks the same path across his world. This is her path home to her son.*

Shatha Wissam, wake up
wake up, my son
we have no more time to think
the city has fled.
I've never seen one road so full of fear
half the city, carrying their homes on their backs
others, go with what family they can find.

Get your things
don't touch the light.
I want to go
before the morning
before the neighbors know
what we have done.

Wissam, my son,
You sleep with my gun?

Wissam Where are people like us?
We used to go through our day
nothing special, only simple.
Now everyone is running
as if we don't belong here.

Shatha Give me my gun.

Wissam The more I look at this gun
the more lost I feel.
Why should I leave
and come back when Iraq is better?

At least Omar's mother sits everyday
in front of her house demanding
the Americans give it back to her.

Shatha Forget this house, Wissam.
All your father's fathers came from Fallujah
but you have not known one of them.
Your father would have welcomed America—

but by America your school is bombed,
your football field
overflowing with bodies of the dead.

Wissam   Since the day I stood in the ashes of my school
I have been without purpose
even without pen and paper.

Everything I was excited to accomplish
collapsed in a second.
Everything I worked for
reduced to the ground.
Where is Uncle Ali's table at the café?
The newspapers I sold outside his store?
I don't want to feel lost anymore.

Who am I without this place?
A refugee?
Not even you would recognize me.

Shatha   We have no other choice
we opened our eyes as old people.

Wissam, today my shoes were covered in bits of flesh.
Today I saw a death so terrifying, it tears you into pieces.
Your feet not where you were last standing
your hands not holding the hands of those you loved.
And worst of all, it can spare you
and take your son instead.

You want me to be the mother, al Khansa?
To talk you into battle?
To praise you for a holy fight?

I am not al Khansa
I do not dream to eulogize your death
to mourn your bravery
or sing over your last breath.

I am not al Khansa
finding honor in revenge
justice in loss
praising God at any cost.

I am not al Khansa
I have no heart for death
for the loss of my only son
for a martyrdom that may never come.

I am not afraid of death
only afraid for you.

Scene Nine

Wissam *leaves his house going out into the street.* **Philip**, *sensing something, crosses silently to his door, closing it. Suddenly, they find themselves together in the same space. If* **Philip** *had a rifle, he might kill Wissam here.*

Philip   Don't move.

Wissam   I'm not armed.

Philip   Then why are you here?

Wissam   I live here.

Phillip   Nobody lives here anymore.
It's where hajis come to fight.

Wissam   I am not armed.

Philip   You don't need to be. You're a kid.
The city's been evacuated.
You shouldn't be here anymore.

Wissam   My mother wants us to leave
our home in your hands.
So I had to know you,
one of you, by name.

Philip   Your own will kill you
just for talking to a marine
they will kill you.

Wissam *risks it.*

Wissam   My name's Wissam.
Wissam, I'll write it for you—

He approaches **Philip**.

Philip   Don't move!

Wissam   Wissam.
And your name?

Philip *doesn't answer.*

Wissam   Your mother named you to mean something—

Philip   I don't even know her name.

Wissam   You don't know your own mother?

Philip   Wissam,
the city's been evacuated.

Tomorrow you won't be seen as a boy
only seen as a threat.

Wissam So you would kill me tomorrow but not today?

Philip This place is gonna be ash.
It's gonna eat through your skin.
Only your clothes will be left.

Wissam Even if I leave
There are more like me.
We are from Fallujah for five hundred years
maybe more.

Philip This is not a home anymore
there is no surviving this.
You've got your mom
you've got your life.

Wissam Better to lose your life
than lose yourself.
It's humiliating
to be defended by someone
who can't speak my language
who is afraid of me.

Phillip We're trying to protect people like you
you're a kid.

Wissam You're a kid.
You don't think in generations
you don't know your family name.

You're an orphan, yes?
You should understand
what it is to be ripped from your home
and everything that made you.

Philip My family didn't make me
my city didn't make me
I made me.

Wissam And war, and war, and war has made me.
We've been surviving so long
maybe we are made from a different mettle than other human beings.

Philip There's no such thing as an innocent kid.

Wissam Innocent? I grew up instantly.

Philip Wissam.
What's your name mean?

Wissam   Medal of honor.

Philip   I hope I don't see you tomorrow, Wissam.

Shatha *finds them together.*

Shatha	**Colleen**
Wissam!	
Wissam!	
	Philip?
	Philip?
Come home	
I want you home.	
Get inside	
close the door	
we can't be here anymore.	
	Just open the door
	let me open the door.
Please, we are leaving.	
	I'm not leaving.
Please we are leaving.	
	Philip,
	Are you listening?
	I can hear you breathing—

Philip   Enough!

Suddenly **Shatha** *and* **Wissam** *are gone.* **Philip** *is in the VA hospital.*

Taylor   Houston, let it go.
Lie down and sleep.
I'll watch the door.

It is hard for **Philip** *to back down. Exhausted, he finally goes to his cot.*

He never sees **Taylor** *once he is dead, only feels an unexplainable comfort.* **Taylor** *gently covers* **Philip** *with a blanket. He stands watch. As soon as* **Philip** *falls asleep, music rages.*

Scene Ten

Kassim *appears out of a shadow, he can go almost anywhere unseen. Perhaps he has been on stage throughout but unnoticed by the marines. There are no boundaries to how he can traverse the space. He knows every corner, he invades* **Philip***'s sleep.*

Wissam *seeks out* **Kassim***. It is here that we make sense of the unspoken relationship we have seen between* **Kassim** *and* **Wissam***.*

Kassim   You're still here? Why?
I thought you would be gone

before the Americans begin their fury.

You are brave to walk in the open
with dead men all around you.
Has the blood of your father
finally begun to flow in your veins?

Wissam   What would you know of my father?

Kassim   I knew him well, Wissam
From our earliest childhood
through school I knew him.
I knew his thoughts
I knew his dreams
I knew him even in his death.
I knew your father longer than your mother knew him,
for fifteen years we were in prison together
tortured together, holding secrets together.
I knew he longed for this day of freedom.
He gave his life for it. For you.

Wissam   My father was tortured by Saddam
He was a simple man
a teacher
he did not carry a gun.

Kassim   I owned a sweet shop
I did not carry a gun.
We fought with words
more dangerous
in a country where you are tortured
for even thinking the truth.

Wissam   Our houses have shared a wall for eighty years
and your only words are
threats to your neighbor's children?
What would my father think of you now?

Kassim   I am sorry, Wissam.
Your father died resisting
but you resist fighting.

All the right people left the fight
and all the wrong people have come to fight.

Would you fight for God?

Wissam   I will not fight by the side of a man
who doesn't know his way to the mosque.

Kassim   Would you fight for your mother?
Where is she now, Wissam?

You have lingered here too long.
If you were afraid, you would have fled.
But here you are
ready
you just don't know what for.

Wissam   I did not stay to fight.

Kassim   When the Americans came,
we shouted our greetings to them.
But when we protested their presence
in the school, they shot us dead.
Their first freedom was
silencing our voices in the street.

Now they shoot anyone walking,
anyone breathing.
I smell my streets rotting.

I saw an old man
one old man
driving with his pick-up truck
full of bodies
all alive.
I asked him where
will you take them?
The hospital is closed and
snipers shoot from the roofs of hospitals.
You're mad to risk your life
for a body, even the mother is too afraid to touch.

He begged my mercy
would I help him lift this one body
onto his truck?

The body was only barely breathing
the flies followed us all the way to the car.
When we finished
he drove past me fast:
"may God bless me a long life"
"a long life"
"a long"—

I tell you I was breathless
I heard a whistle
and felt my feet leave the ground.
The air in my lungs so tight
I thought I was a ghost.
The old man, his truck, his bodies
covered the street.

The body blown all the way back to where
we picked it from the dirt.
But now it was in pieces,
the pieces were on me.

You are right
you cannot carry a gun, Wissam,
you cannot shoot one or two
of the thousands who take our city.
But you can carry a message
with your innocence
your gentle face.

Wissam   You want me to martyr myself for you?

Kassim   Not for me—

Wissam, Fallujah is suicide.
So why did you stay
if not to be your father's son?

Scene Eleven

Philip *sits up fast as if from a nightmare.*

Lalo   Man up!

It's cleared hot.
The whole of Fallujah
door to door.

Rocks   We're doing what?

Lalo   Purging the city.

Rocks   That's death.

Philip   It's why three hundred thousand people
fled this place.

Lalo   Most people are out.
Anyone left
is a target
and perceived as a threat.
New ROE
shoot anything that moves.

Even if you think you've got the area
memorized in your head
they've dug tunnels and trenches
put jersey barriers inside houses

bricked over doors to rooftops
so don't get stuck,
the streets are narrow, the houses are worse.

Line up.
I want your calls home
say your goodbyes.

Don't tip your hands too much.

The men line up for final calls home to their family.

Rocks   Hey, Dad
how are you?
Fine, it's fine—
I'm bored out of my mind.
How's Mom?
She's not home?
Okay.
Yeah, I'll
call back.
I don't know
maybe
later.
So.
How's my dog?

Well tell Mom,
tell her,
tell her,

Corpsman   It's me
Just calling to see how you are, Mom.

It's hot
and hot.

Damn,
could you just for once
not ask me
how many.
Don't watch the news.

I'm sorry you can't sleep.

Lalo   Hey, love
how are you?
I'm fine.
How's school?

Don't get distracted
put your head down and study.

I got the baby wipes, I got the chocolate.
It was awesome
I'm listening to that song all the time now.

I don't know
maybe some chicken cacciatore or something
and some magazines
or some new underwear
I need new underwear.

Rocks   I love her
and
and
and
and I love you, Dad
and
I'm so
fortunate
to be
your son.

Corpsman   Why did I even call?
They should be trained in what not to say for Christ sake.
I'm worried about getting killed
but more worried I'm killing my mom.

Lalo   Don't worry
I'm just running around in the desert
playing with scorpions.

I'm always there
with you.

Philip *steps forward and stands center; he is silent.*

Colleen   Philip?
Philip?

I know it's you—
I woke today dreaming you—

Shatha *puts a woman's abaya over* **Wissam** *to disguise his identity.*

Wissam   I look like I'm hiding

Shatha   You have to hide
they won't let boys out of the city—

Wissam   Leave it now
just say goodbye.

Shatha   How do I say goodbye to the walls of my life?
My husband's garden?

The bed where you were born?

Wissam Just say goodbye, *yumma*.

Philip, Rocks, Lalo, Corpsman, Shatha and Wissam
Goodbye.

Shatha Do I lock the door?

Philip, Rocks, Lalo, Corpsman
Ooh rah!

The marines take the stage as if going door to door, **Philip** *on point.*

Kassim *enters* **Wissam**'s *house from a neighboring rooftop looking for a place to hide.*

Kassim Where are you going in your mother's robe?

How humiliating, you
dressed as a woman
with marines coming door to door.

Wissam Goodbye, Kassim!

Kassim Syrians, Libyans, Chechens all here to fight,
and you, running from your own country?

Wissam I can fight you just by walking in the street.

Defiant, he steps out into the open exposing himself. **Shatha**, *terrified, runs after him.* **Philip** *feels the abaya brush past him traversing the same path as in previous scenes.*

Philip Enough!

In one excited and deft movement he kills **Shatha** *with his ka-bar.* **Shatha**'s *body crumples to the ground.*

Wissam *Youm ruddi! Youm ruddi!*

Philip *is about to kill* **Wissam**.

Wissam *Ya waylee yumma ya waylee!*

Lalo Lite her up!

Wissam *Youm ruddi!*

Colleen Philip! Philip! I woke today dreaming you—

Philip *suddenly recognizes* **Wissam**.

Philip CORPSMAN UP!

Corpsman She's playing possum!

Philip I know him.

86   Fallujah

Colleen   Philip, I can't hear you breathing.

Scene Twelve

Shatha, *now dead, rises, letting her abaya fall to the floor behind her.*

Lalo, Rocks, Corpsman   On behalf of the marine corps
we regret to inform you that your son

Shatha   *Yumma weledi, yumma weledi.*
ya waylee yabni ya waylee.

At a loss, **Wissam** *looks around for his mother's dead body.*

Wissam   She is in pieces.

Shatha   *Yumma weledi, yumma weledi.*

Will no one help him? **Wissam** *collapses on the floor over his mother's abaya.* **Philip** *and* **Wissam** *are both isolated and alone.*

Colleen How can I talk to him?	
How can I care for him?	**Shatha** How can I care for him?
	Wissam How can I bury her?
It hurts him to be mine.	**Shatha** It hurt him to be mine
His eyes, his chin, his skin	His beautiful eyes, his father's chin, his pure, pure skin
came from another mother	came from his father.
but in my heart he's mine	
it's my belief	His brave belief.
I feel his grief.	His endless grief.
I made a fighter	
from a frightened boy.	
They said he couldn't heal or feel	
but I saw who he was	I saw who he was
who he was	who he was
was my job.	was Wissam.
	Since the day I became a mother
	my compass turned only
	in the direction of you.
How many times he tried	
to take his life?	
I had to keep the boy alive—	
	But now we are in pieces
	in pieces.

He was in pieces.
The kind of love he wanted
would have made him my son.
It would not have made him a man.

I needed him to be someone
anyone but lost.

       Wissam I'm an orphan to everything.

       Kassim Here you are ready, now you know what for.

Rocks And war, and war and war has made me.

       Wissam This is not a home anymore.

       Kassim And war, and war and war has made me.

Taylor Asking where I am
and who I am,
and who I'm gonna be when I get home.

Colleen I knew who he was,
we all did

       Shatha Who he was
       was as old as his country.

I knew
he grew up instantly.

So what choice did I have? **Wissam** So what choice did I have?

       Wissam & Shatha We opened our eyes as
       old people.

But to lose the boy.
Lose the boy.

Corpsman There is no such thing as an innocent kid.

Lalo No one comes back to the same family.

       Shatha I am now al Khansa
       Wissam & Shatha with a heart full of death
       Shatha for the loss of my only son.
       Wissam For a peace that will never come.
       Peace that will never come.

Colleen So his job has just begun.
Now leave me alone with my son.

The cast begin to exit leaving **Colleen** *with her son.*

Rocks Nobody's gonna know who he is.

Corpsman   His face is gone.

Taylor   Take your boot off his head.

Kassim   We've been here before.

Lalo   He's playing possum.

Kassim   The body blown back to where we picked it from the dirt.

Taylor   Did she cry when you almost died?

Shatha   Then she's your mother.

Suddenly **Colleen** *steps through the door to* **Philip**'s *room at the VA hospital.*

Scene Thirteen

Philip *sits up fast, as if from a nightmare.*

Philip   CORPSMAN UP!

Corpsman   Philip, your mom—

Philip   I can't—

Corpsman   She thought you were dead
gets a suicide call.

Philip   I can't—

Corpsman   Look at her!

Philip   I'm not back!
I'm numb, scared—
Don't drink
don't leave the house
wearing earphones everywhere
music
my only company
only music can keep me
keep me in
keep me
keep me back
back inside
where it hurts
let me hurt!
Hurt myself back from numb.

He hits himself so hard, he finally catches a breath.

How can I talk to her?
How can I care for her?

It hurts her
it hurts her
to be mine.
How can I?
How can I hurt her?

Corpsman   I'll be outside.
I'll watch the door.

He exits leaving the door open. **Philip** *and* **Colleen** *are finally alone.*

Scene Fourteen

Colleen	**Philip**
We've been here before.	
	Buried alive.
We've both been here before	
trying to survive	Trying to survive.
but this time I won't cry	
I won't look away	
I will listen	
listen.	

I found you before
I gave you something to fight for.
What keeps you awake
keeps you alive.
I am vigilant
vigilant.

My mind
is a minefield of you.
I don't sleep
this year you've been back.
I read.
I watch.
I listen.

I'm not afraid of what you've become.
I know you'll find the same in me
a numb nerve
can't eat, can't care, can't see
other people smiling—
I won't cry.
I won't ask.
I will listen
listen.

I will not close my eyes
to what you've seen
or who you are
or who you are going to be.

How can I sleep seeing what you see?
This war has made a monster of me.

Philip Mom,
I had a boy
I had his mother
in my hands—
and he was so much more than me
so much more
and I killed her with my bare hands.
So, Mom, what does that make me?

Beat.

Colleen I won't ask.
I won't look away.
I will listen.
I will listen.

Philip Listen—

Wissam My name's Wissam.
Wissam, I'll write it for you,

*He closes the door to **Philip**'s room and writes his name in Arabic across the back of it.*

Wissam Wissam.
And your name?
Your mother named you to mean something.

End of Opera

Noura

Playwrights Horizons, Inc. in association with Shakespeare Theatre Company produced the New York premiere of *Noura* in 2018

World premiere produced by Shakespeare Theatre Company
Artistic Director: Michael Kahn
Executive Director: Chris Jennings

Originally workshopped and developed with the Laboratory for Global Performance and Politics at Georgetown University in the Davis Performing Arts Center, directed by Derek Goldman and dramaturgy by Maya E. Roth.

Noura was further developed at McCarter Theatre Center within their LAB play development programs and was produced by McCarter in Princeton, NJ as the 2017 LAB Spotlight Production. Emily Mann, Artistic Director, Timothy J. Shields, Managing Director.

Characters

Sometimes characters are referred to by their Iraqi names, sometimes by the names they took when immigrating to America.

Noura/Nora *An architect. Originally from Mosul, Iraq. Now an immigrant living in New York City. (Mid- to late forties.)*

Tareq/Tim *Noura's husband. Charismatic and gentle. A former surgeon, originally from Baghdad. Now a hospitalist working in an E.R. in New York. (Mid- to late forties.)*

Rafa'a *Noura's childhood neighbor from Mosul. A close friend of the family and a surrogate uncle to Yazen. Elegant and private. An OBGYN. (Mid- to late forties.)*

Maryam *A young physicist from Mosul. Now in her first semester of graduate studies in California. Unapologetic. (Mid-twenties.)*

Yazen/Alex *Noura and Tareq's son. Intelligent and astute but still a boy. Very American. (Eleven–fourteen years old.)*

Noura's family are Christian Iraqi and Rafa'a is a Muslim Iraqi.

Notes

The set is an expression of Noura's world as an architect. The set can breathe and manifest as her conscious and unconscious needs manifest. There is a larger than expected dining table; it accommodates everything.

There is also a simple but magnificent Christmas tree. Presents beneath it. The rest is sparse. Perhaps minimalist. Perhaps they haven't quite moved in.

A (/) indicates a cue for the next character to speak, cutting off the line before.

A (—) indicates a character cutting themselves off, or in search of finishing their thought.

Truth is a pathless land.

—*Krishnamurti*

Scene One

Outdoors, cold. **Noura** *wears a blanket or winter coat over her pajamas.*

When she thinks her mind speaks aloud. We hear her secret thoughts throughout the play. Sometimes they come as a cacophony of whispers in Arabic, sometimes as tangential thoughts. We hear phrases of the Hail Mary in Arabic dropping softly, then she takes a breath.

Silence.

Noura Is it silent? Snow?

If it is silent, it is the loudest silence I have ever heard.

I felt snow once. On the coldest day in Mosul. Blessed mother, you came like a friend.

We wait for so long, forget how to dream, then a door opens

or closes—

Now, everything is possible again.

She laughs.

Tareq Are you awake?

Nora?

He teases her, over-pronouncing her name.

Darling Nora.

Scene Two

Inside.

Noura You're hoping I answer to that name, so you put a darling with it.

Tareq *Habibti*, your passport now says Nora.

Noura You changed my name against my will—call me by my real name.

Tareq It's hardly any different / no one

Noura Then why change it?

Tareq I love Nora.

Noura Say it right, nobody ever said it as sweet as you.

Tareq Oh I see. *Noura*, when I need something sweet from you, sing *Noura* in your ear.

Noura Yes like this.

Tareq   *Noura*, let's make a baby.

Noura   Oh my God. Now?

Tareq   Now. Here. On the table. On top of our passports. I want an American baby, with your eyes and my incredible ability to cook. One that smells like you and fights like you but has my sweet disposition.

Noura   So sweet. Is Yazen still sleeping?

Tareq   I want a girl. To dress up and smell good.

Noura   Is that sexist?

Tareq   Or selfish. Our son can't lift his head from the computer long enough to see I'm turning grey. She'll be a physician, look after us in our old age. Nothing sexist about that. It's honorable.

Kiss me, Noura.

She shoves an electric toothbrush in her mouth instead.

Talking while brushing her teeth:

Noura   Which for Yazen? Backgammon or Legos?

Tareq   He wants PlayStation so he can be like other boys.

Noura   It's violent.

Tareq   Boys here don't play backgammon. Let's at least give him the Lego guys with guns, we can't keep him innocent forever, it's just play.

She sings his name:

Noura   Tareq.

Tareq   *Noura.*

She kisses him now that her teeth are brushed.

Tareq   You told me you stopped smoking.

Noura   It's Christmas.

Beat.

Tareq   You know why I love Christmas?

He whispers something in her ear.

Noura   You have a surprise for me?

She reaches for her iPhone/Facebook then shows him the screen.

Noura   Just look at her.

Tareq   How long is she staying?

Noura   She didn't say. It's her winter break.

Tareq   Are we going to take her in?

Silence.

How? You won't even buy a couch. I know you want to sponsor every Iraqi orphan. Once we open that door, you know it will never close.

Noura   Not every orphan, one. From Mosul. From my grandfather's church.

Tareq   She can't bring Mosul back.

Noura   She's lucky to be alive. The least we can do is help with her school.

Tareq   I need distance.

Noura   From what?

Tareq   Tomorrow will be beautiful, we'll feed her. Over-feed her. Then follow her on Facebook.

Noura   She'll stay a week, at most two. She's got school. In California. You might like having a girl around the house / you just said

Tareq   This generation, they're hard, they're refugees. I just want to prepare / you

Noura   We're refugees.

Tareq   She's not family.

Scene Three

Rafa'a *buzzes then lets himself in.*

Noura   Here we go!   **Tareq**   Yazen!

Noura *quickly exits to get dressed for the day. Both men watch her go.*

Rafa'a (*to* **Tareq**)   Shh! Wait, wait!

Yazen!

Yazen *enters.*

Yazen   Rafa'a! I thought you couldn't /

Rafa'a   What's today?

Yazen   Errands in the morning, then I pick the movie.

Rafa'a   No. What day is today?

Yazen   Christmas Eve.

Rafa'a   And what did I promise I would put in your hand on Christmas eve?

He triumphantly holds up a hard drive.

Ta da! Downloaded! Straight from the Cloud. All of it.

Tareq (*to* **Rafa'a**)   Is the data good? Did you check?

Rafa'a It's here.

He presents the hard drive to **Yazen**.

Yazen That's it?

Rafa'a It's EVERYTHING. One terabyte. Straight from Mosul!

Yazen How? Someone got into Grandpa's house again?

Rafa'a Not someone, our old neighbor. I told him, this time, photograph every page of every book in her house. Now all of it is here.

Tareq Noura's been talking about her library for more than a decade!

Rafa'a Wait until you see the picture of her mother he found stuck in a book. *Mashallah*. I was in and out of her house my whole life and I never saw a picture of her mother.

Tareq I want to give it to her right now!

Rafa'a There's more . . . a day or two later the neighbor was paid to burn every book on our street. And he did it. The same guy.

Yazen Why?

Rafa'a Why what?

Yazen Why would the neighbor burn Mom's books?

Rafa'a He was paid.

Yazen But you know him.

Rafa'a Yes. He burned my books too.

Yazen Just for money?

Tareq No, Alex—

Beat.

Yazen He still sent you the file.

Rafa'a At great risk. Encrypted on Telegram. Noura's entire family library—all from the Cloud!

Yazen All in my hand!

(*To* **Rafa'a**.) What about your books?

Rafa'a I'll read your mother's.

The men hear **Noura** *enter.*

Yazen Morning, Nunu!

Tareq Shhh, Alex. Wrap this, for tomorrow.

Noura *begins breakfast/tea where* **Tareq** *left off.*

Tareq   So Shark Tank?!

Rafa'a   I see why you're addicted.

Tareq   We have to go into business! Forget medicine.

Rafa'a   Medicine is business.

Tareq   But I want to invent something!

Rafa'a   Something medical?

Tareq   No. In restaurants / I've seen

Yazen   They have that already, Dad.

Tareq   Not in homes. If the markets hold, in three years / I could build

Noura   Toast and tea.

Noura *arrives carrying a tray.*

Tareq   Alex, move the books please.

Noura   I'll move them later.

Tareq *attempts to move her renderings.*

Tareq   How can we eat with your mess all over the table?

Noura   You'll rearrange my mind if you touch them.

Tareq   I'll buy you a desk.

Yazen   She never leaves things in the same place.

Noura   My desk is in my mind. I have organization you cannot see. (*She prays*) "Blessed God, thank you that we even have food, if we eat off books, it's more than millions of refugees have, make us grateful lord. Amen."

Rafa'a (*to himself*)   Bismullah. Il Rahman al Rahim.

Beat.

What's all this? Still re-designing Baghdad?

Noura   I'm thinking to stop tutoring.

Tareq   You don't need to work. My income could double now that I'm a citizen!

Yazen   She can't stop working.

Tareq   Why? What do you know?

Yazen   I saw her drawing—equations all over the margins—it looked like Noah's Ark.

He starts to unroll one of the sketches on the table.

Noura   Stop snooping.

Yazen   Mom, it was in my room /

Noura It's wherever I can find space to think.

Yazen On my homework?

Noura I work at your desk some days when you're at school.

Yazen Then don't get mad if I look through your stuff.

Noura It's not an ark, Yazen. (*To* **Rafa'a**.) Yes, I would like to stop tutoring.

Rafa'a Go back to being an architect. Take the A.R.E.

Noura I thought you were on your way to a birth?

Rafa'a The baby came. In a cab.

Tareq You still get paid for that?

Rafa'a My first Face Time delivery! Now I'm free for errands / like you hoped.

Tareq Thank / God.

Noura Are you bringing Kate tomorrow?

Rafa'a No.

Yazen Dara?

Rafa'a No.

Yazen Who are you bringing to Christmas?

Rafa'a I thought I would just come myself.

Noura We've been cooking / for three weeks.

Tareq Twice as much food as last / year.

Noura Think about bringing someone, Rafa'a. Just a friend.

Yazen I miss Reem.

Tareq Reem moved back to London.

Yazen But /

Tareq Enough.

Yazen Mom, I'm starving.

Noura Yazen, you can do it.

Yazen I need more than toast /

Noura When we break our fast tonight you will feel / so strong.

Tareq Give the boy an egg.

Noura He's old enough to understand.

Tareq Suffering?

Noura Compassion. It's Christmas Eve. We fast.

She pulls out her iPhone/Facebook.

Tareq Alex, love, go get your shoes on. I don't want to have to rush.

Tareq, **Yazen**, *and* **Rafa'a** *prepare to leave.*

Rafa'a You're gonna need boots, Yazen.

Noura *still on her phone.*

Noura (*to* **Rafa'a**) Whoever she is, you can bring her.

Yazen She needs more people to eat all the food.

Noura You can invite someone too, Yazen.

Tareq (*over* **Noura**'*s shoulder*) Please stop watching that stuff. Forget it.

Tareq *whispers in her ear. It brings her up for air.*

Noura It's evening in Baghdad soon – it's already Christmas in New Zealand, we have to call your sister when you / get back before

Tareq Give everyone my love. I'll call Nadia while I'm out. (*To* **Yazen**) Here, a cheesestick. Because it's already Christmas in New Zealand!

Noura We have to post something before they leave for Mass. They need to know we're thinking about them.

Tareq, **Rafa'a**, *and* **Yazen** *exit.*

Yazen Bye, Mom!

Noura Quick, Yazen, here, in front of the tree. Hide your cheesestick.

She takes his picture with her phone.

You get to meet Maryam tomorrow.

Yazen Is she the nun?

Noura A nun? No. Why?

Yazen You said she lived in a convent.

Noura As an orphan. She grew up there. The nuns were her mommies.

Yazen Does she like PlayStation?

Noura She's probably never seen one.

Yazen *makes a sound of disappointment.*

Noura Love you.   **Yazen** Love you.

Yazen *exits.* **Noura** *finishes posting* **Yazen**'*s photo.*

Finally, **Noura** *is alone.*

Silence.

She thinks visually.

She studies the dining table, adjusts something, likely a chair. She wraps up in her blanket and steps outside.

Scene Four

She lights a cigarette. A deep inhale.

Noura   I need more chairs. For tomorrow.

A touch of snow begins to fall. Magic.

Men want to make babies till they're eighty—

A young woman approaches **Noura**. *She wears an overstuffed backpack and carries some shopping parcels.* **Noura** *in her own world. Then—*

Noura   Oh God! Oh love, Maryam?! What are you doing here? Today?

Maryam   We get to meet. Finally.

Noura   Maryam! Little darling! How could I not recognize you? I've been staring at your beautiful "face book." You're different. What, you've been eating your way through America?!

Please come / in.

Maryam   No, finish your cigarette. I don't mind, I've never seen snow before.

Noura   Not in Mosul? Of course not, it's your first winter in America!

Maryam   It's magnificent. The nuns described it, but we couldn't imagine snow.

Noura   Taste it.

Maryam   What?!

Noura *sticks her tongue out to catch a snow flake.* **Maryam** *follows.*

Maryam   I thought I would hate the cold but I think the opposite, I think I love it.

Noura   It's anonymous.

Maryam   How?

Noura   In the heat, everybody knows your business. What you're wearing, how you walk. In the cold nobody cares. You can go anywhere in your own world.

She catches herself staring.

Elhamdullah ya binti.

Maryam   Shukran ya Noura.

Noura Come in! Come in!

She puts out her cigarette.

No more messaging, you're finally here in person.

Maryam The ticket was too much really.

Noura Next time I'll come to California.

They enter the home. **Maryam** *stays just inside the doorway. She knows her way out before she steps into a room.*

Maryam Wow!

Noura What?

Maryam It's empty. I mean modern. Most / Iraqis

Noura I know, the curly furniture.

Maryam You're an architect, right?

Beat.

You stopped?

Noura Can I take your coat?

Maryam *moves directly toward a photo.*

Maryam Your family?

Noura My father as a boy. And this, do you recognize? Sister Rana.

Maryam My head mother? As a girl?

Noura Before the convent, she was engaged to my father.   **Maryam** What?

Noura But she wanted to become a nun. So, years later, he married her little sister instead. This one, with her head turned, defiant. My mother.

Maryam Sister Rana was your aunt?

Noura She wanted me to become a nun.

Maryam Of course, it's her mission. She was my world.

Noura She talked of you. We spoke each month for twenty-six years.

Maryam Her death was unspeakable. I'm sorry. I was there.

Silence.

Noura What's this?

She refers to the parcels **Maryam** *is still carrying.*

Maryam Presents for your son. Yazen? Sorry, I should have texted / first

Noura Of course not, this is your home. Open the refrigerator, eat, eat everything, don't ask, just be at home. Where's your suitcase?

Maryam *shrugs. She continues to look through the apartment.*

Maryam   I'm staying with a friend from school.

Noura   A friend? Why not stay here?

Beat.

It's good you've made friends. I was so lonely at first.

How long have you been here?

Maryam   A week.

Noura   And you didn't call me?

Beat.

What a blessing you are! Maryam, I have so much I want to tell / you! We

Maryam *picks something up off the dining table.*

Maryam   You have American passports?

Noura   They just came this week!

Look, Alex, Tim and Nora. It took eight years. I can't tell you the pressure, Tareq was working at Subway sandwich, can you believe it? A surgeon working in a kitchen. He's in E.R. now, not surgery, but, it's coming together, I'm happy! Today, I'm like a girl again.

How's the dorm?

Maryam   Great.

Noura   I thought having girls around—I looked for a group—I mean to go from a convent to California. I looked for a Catholic school, so you would feel more comfortable, but no, you / wanted

Maryam   Stanford's great.

Noura   Yes, it is. I'll make tea.

Maryam   How did you even find me?

Noura   You mean on Facebook?

Maryam   I never use my last name.

Noura   I looked at every Maryam from Mosul. To make sure you escaped.

Beat.

Maryam   Sister Rana talked about me?

Noura   *Habibti.* Tell me, you posted about an internship?

Maryam   Yes, weapons contracts. I started working on a proof of concept, I mean it started as just theory when I was in Iraq but, then the D.O.D. awarded me this internship and have hinted at a job after I graduate.

Noura   But you're studying physics?

Maryam   Yes. Thermodynamics.

Noura   Why the military?

Maryam   They pay people to do physics.

Noura   How will you stay after your student visa?

Maryam   The D.O.D. could hire me.

Noura   Even now? Visas are impossible. We just this month got our citizenship, it took eight years.

Maryam   I'm not worried.

Noura   I'll make tea.

She goes to put the kettle on.

Maryam   What are you working on? The drawings?

Noura   Oh, it's a house, for Tareq. You can open them—

It's a fantasy. For his family. To live all together, like the old houses, with a garden in the middle. He wants apartments for his five sisters, they all have kids, it'd be impossible to build.

Maryam   Why impossible?

Noura   There's forty-three of them. And, this is modern, more like a ship—

She walks her through the renderings.

The lower level, a huge communal kitchen, bedrooms going all the way up to the roof. On the ground floor, each family's sitting room opens to the courtyard, so on big occasions if you open the interior doors, it makes a giant circular room. I wanted all Mouslawi marble, like this piece, going inside to out.

Maryam   To keep cool.

Noura   I don't know—

Maryam   What?

Noura   With the garden at the center, to get from room to room, you travel around the courtyard, so the daily pattern is circular, right?

Maryam   I see.

Noura   So the family stays connected to each other and private from the street. But aren't they isolated? All the life is inside, behind walls. If you're not in the family, it's inaccessible.

Maryam   Nobody builds courtyard houses anymore.

Noura   They do in Paris. It's the latest trend. Have you seen in some parts of America, they have yards? They use grass. It touches the neighbor's grass—without a boundary.

Maryam To build there? Here?

Noura Nowhere. It's for his imagination. He still wants to provide for his sisters.

Maryam Where are his sisters?

Noura Scattered. Germany, New Zealand, Sweden.

Beat.

Maryam In Baghdad they're tearing down homes. You don't even buy the house anymore. You just buy the land. Like in Dubai.

Noura We can't live in Baghdad.

She goes to finish making tea. **Maryam** *looks at the books. If she opens one, she leaves it exactly as she found it.*

Noura You must be a genius if they want you for a job already!

Maryam I translated for so many U.S. contractors in Mosul. But thank God for your sponsorship. I couldn't have afforded it / otherwise.

She takes off her coat. She is visibly pregnant.

Noura Of course we're fasting today, but tomorrow we've cooked everything Mouslawi. Tareq's from Baghdad, so we usually do both. But for you, I wanted only Mouslawi—

She sees **Maryam** *is pregnant.*

Beat.

Noura You must be hungry.

Maryam Don't worry—I'm fine.

Noura I'll make something.

She tries to go.

Maryam I don't want food.

Noura Breakfast, lunch, something—

Maryam I don't need.

Noura *goes anyway.*

Silence.

She returns with nothing.

Noura I'm sorry. Are you okay? Who did this?

Maryam Nobody, I'm / fine

Noura It happened in Mosul?

Maryam I'm only six months. Maybe I should have mentioned it first.

Noura   It happened here? Did you tell the police?

They arrest people here / take their DNA.

Maryam   Noura, I'm just pregnant, I wanted the baby.

Noura   You got married?

Maryam   I chose to have a baby, not a husband, a baby.

Noura   I've been talking to Iraqis, engineers, men with citizenship. They won't marry / you now

Maryam   I don't want to get married. I have school, my whole life.

Noura   How? You can't just do that.

Beat.

Maryam   Sorry, but I don't see it that way. Come on, I don't have to explain to you. *Daesh*, when you see them face to face.

I'm an orphan, I want someone of my own.

Noura   You have total freedom now, I never had, how are you going to—

A child can't save you, Maryam. You don't know.

Maryam   Everyone I know is a refugee, or dead.

Noura   Exactly, why bring a child into this world?

Maryam   I'm alone.

I've never been so alone. In Iraq, there are people, all the / time.

Noura   But you can't go back home now, unmarried, with a child, you won't be accepted.

Maryam   Are you kidding? Would you go back? To Mosul? It's gone. The people are unrecognizable.

You wouldn't survive a day in Mosul now.

Silence.

Whispers overwhelm **Noura** *and fill the room with Arabic gossip*: (*Ha'tha Eeb*), (*Kan El-Mafroudh Et'sa'qoudou El-Dhe'fil*), (*Rah Ten'Qa'til*)

Maryam   Are you alright?

Noura   You felt alone? Why didn't you call me?

Maryam   I can see now I make you really uncomfortable. God, you've been out almost eight years. You live in New York, your husband works at a hospital. I didn't know you were going to be so old world. You seemed progressive online.

Noura   Old world? What does that even mean? I tutor math in an inner-city high school, I'm not naive. You were raised in a convent. I'm just surprised, you don't, you're not, shy.

Maryam I'm not embarrassed, no. I've been stared at my whole life. Every girl without a father is.

Okay, forget it. Look, those are presents, for Yazen, you said he was eleven? Thirteen? Anyway, I'll leave them here, they were too big to carry back on the subway, that's why I dropped by.

Noura Where are you staying?

Maryam With my classmate. Up. Somewhere. The Bronx.

Noura You won't stay here?

Maryam I'm already there.

Noura You would rather stay with your friend?

Maryam Please can you give them to Yazen for Christmas?

Noura You are still coming for Christmas dinner?

Maryam Why don't I text you.

Noura You are still coming. You have to. Spend the day, the week.

Maryam Let's text, see how it goes.

Noura We are all expecting you.

Maryam I'm not sure you were expecting *me*.

Noura Please come, you must come. We are your family, while you are here.

Maryam We'll see.

She leaves.

Noura *is unmoored. A terrifying silence.*

Scene Five

Rafa'a *enters with an armful of presents.* **Noura** *doesn't notice him.*

Rafa'a Noura?

Noura We didn't even begin, and she's finished?

Rafa'a Hello?

Noura *jumps.*

Noura You scared me.

Rafa'a Don't you feel the cold? Your door's open.

Noura She left the door open?

Rafa'a Who?

Beat.

What's wrong?

Noura Who can talk without tea?

Rafa'a I'll make it.

Noura Everything straight to the point—I feel beaten up.

Rafa'a Have you seen a ghost?

Noura No.

I don't know.

I've seen Maryam.

Rafa'a From Mosul?

Noura She came early, from California.

Rafa'a Good! She's all you talk about.

Noura There was nothing. No conversation, no tea.

Rafa'a She's American already?

Noura Don't make fun.

Rafa'a Maybe she likes coffee?

Noura The way she talks! She didn't compliment me once.

Rafa'a OK. What did she say?

Noura I don't know. She wants something of "her own."

Rafa'a At least she came! This is great. Noura?

Silence.

Noura She's pregnant.

Rafa'a Oh.

Noura She's not married.

Rafa'a No? (*Beat.*) That's all?

Noura That's all?

There's nothing worse! Tareq will reject her outright. She's meant to come for Christmas, all the Mouslawi food, I wanted her to stay, for summers, be part of our family. He goes on and on, he wants a full house, a daughter, babies. Now, she's pregnant.

Rafa'a That sounds perfect for him.

Noura Can she even come for dinner now? What will I say?

Rafa'a What do you want to say?

Noura She's got slut written all over her.

Rafa'a Whoa! Do you hear yourself? Why are you so worried about Tareq rejecting her? You've rejected her already.

Noura I haven't.

Rafa'a You've just described in one word you find her shameful.

Noura Isn't she?

Rafa'a Are you asking me?

Noura I am.

Rafa'a Depends on what you think of shame. Is being pregnant shameful?

Noura Don't turn this into a medical argument, not today. I'm trying to hold myself together, okay? I wanted to welcome her, she shows up pregnant and unapologetic.

Rafa'a So it's the lack of apology? It's okay to be pregnant if you are sorry?

Noura If Tareq rejects her, that's it. It's over.

Rafa'a That doesn't mean she shouldn't come. It might be good for both of you to sit with a young Iraqi refugee over Christmas. I can't think of anything more "Christmassy." Welcoming into your home a pregnant woman who has no place to go.

Back in a bit.

He exits.

Noura *sits with herself.*

A revelation. **Noura** *rearranges something. Then grabs her purse and coat and leaves the house.*

Scene Six

Noura *alone battling PlayStation aggressively and with utter release.*

Noura I've got it, I've got it . . . YES!

Tareq PlayStation?!

Noura It's *Borderlands*! I bought all new presents. One of my students got me started. He says I'm a natural!

Tareq What? *Borderlands*!?

Noura It's a surprise!

Tareq A huge surprise, it's the most violent / game.

Noura We're too protective. He asks about violence. What am I supposed to tell him?

Tareq Tell him the truth.

Noura ISIS are selling girls your age and sawing off the heads of your neighbors?

Tareq He's American now, Nora.

Noura So is ISIS.

She ends the game. She puts the PlayStation joystick into a festive box under the tree.

Tareq *trying to delay, finally goes to put on his lanyard.*

Noura About dinner tomorrow, Maryam—

I thought you weren't working today?

Tareq Night shift.

Noura Mass is at night. You used to always get Christmas / off.

Tareq You want me home for Christmas *Habibti*? Not only will I be here, I will be home before your eyes open and on the pillow next to you will be my gift.

He whispers something in her ear.

Noura Hmm.

Tareq What does my Numi like? What can I find to make your heart dance?

Noura Nothing, I don't need anything.

Tareq Not what you need, what do you want?

Noura I want nothing you could possibly buy at eight o'clock on Christmas Eve. A present is something you plan, with thought, not going to the store the night before and buying the first thing you see. I don't like those kinds of presents. They feel obligatory. You never plan for me. So then you buy something too extravagant to make up / for it.

Tareq You might have to wait until tomorrow to find out.

Noura We need flour before / tomorrow.

Tareq I bought fifteen pounds / a few weeks ago?

Noura I've been baking *claecha* all month—for Yazen's teachers, the school, neighbors, we have hardly any left.

He cuddles up to her.

Tareq *Noura*, did you plan a present for me? Or are you just going to stuff me with cookies?

Noura Maybe.

Tareq Want to know what I want?

Beat.

Noura A daughter.

Tareq How did you guess?

Noura Who smells like me and cooks like you.

Tareq You do know.

Noura My love, about tomorrow, Maryam / she's not

Tareq We're used to big families, doesn't this feel empty to you?

Noura You feel empty?

Tareq No. I feel safe for the first time in my life. It feels so different to feel safe.

He kisses her. She showers him with affection. He stops. She is left wondering.

A whisper of Arabic comes into the room.

Noura There's something I want to tell you.

Tareq What?

Silence.

Noura Is there something I need to know?

Tareq Like what?

Noura After all these years insisting we have only one child?

Tareq Noura, our circumstances were different / we couldn't afford

Noura I mean since we've been in America. Six, seven years ago you didn't even hint.

Tareq I was barely earning /

Noura I'm old enough to be a grandmother.

Tareq In New York that's when women start trying.

Noura My body is / different.

Tareq I don't want to regret having one child. I had five sisters. I need a girl.

Noura Well, raising a girl here is different from back home. She's not going to grow up like your sisters.

Tareq I never thought I would be lonely. It's the hardest thing about being here.

Noura Tomorrow you won't be lonely. You'll see. It might be the most beautiful Christmas we've ever had.

They hold each other. It is love and decades of partnership.

Tareq What is it you wanted to tell me?

Is it the right time?

Noura *wraps up in her blanket and collapses on the floor in front of the Christmas tree.*

Noura   Ten minutes.

She cat naps. **Tareq** *prepares to leave, then watches her again. He sets an alarm on her iPhone.* **Rafa'a** *and* **Yazen** *return from the movies.*

Tareq   I've set the alarm so she doesn't sleep through mass.

Yazen *proudly hands* **Tareq** *a very small exquisitely wrapped jewelry box.*

Yazen (*whispering*)   Here, I wrapped the hard drive for Mom.

Tareq   Oh, love! It doesn't look like her whole library, does it?

Yazen   It looks like jewelry. She's gonna flip.

Tareq   She's gonna flip.

Tareq *kisses* **Yazen**.

Rafa'a   You trying to avoid mass?

Tareq   A half-shift. The money was triple.

Rafa'a   You can always ask /

Tareq   What?

Beat.

Rafa'a   Let me drive you. You'll spend half the night on the bus.

The men leave together. **Yazen** *tucks the jewelry box in the tree then snuggles into his mom on the floor. He plays a video game on her iPhone.*

Scene Seven

Time passes. A song begins somewhere in the house then drifts away. Maybe she is dreaming it. Perhaps the phone alarm goes off. **Yazen** *snuggles in closer. She gently pats him or strokes his hair. She sits thinking.*

Noura *hums a lullaby in Aramaic. Then stops. Silence.*

Noura   Who do I love?

Yazen   Me.

Noura   Who else do I love?

Yazen   Daddy. Nanna. All our family. All over the world.

Noura   Who the most?

Yazen   Me.

Silence.

Noura   What are you thinking? I can feel your brain moving.

Yazen   About tomorrow. Morning.

Noura   Your presents?

Yazen   Mmm.

Noura   Do you think you'll have any presents under the tree?

Yazen   Lots!

Noura   No! Why lots?

Yazen   Because you love me lots.

Noura   That's true! But what do presents have to do with how much I love you?

Yazen   Nothing. They're just fun, Mom. And you like giving presents even if you give too much.

Noura   Well, I could return some of them.

Yazen   Mom!

Shhh. Stop talking.

You can pat my head. And sing that song.

He snuggles in closer.

Yazen   You like surprises?

Noura   Mmm.

Yazen   You thinking about tomorrow?

Noura   I've been thinking about this day a long time.

Beat.

Yazen   Did you wrap the new house for Dad?

Noura   It's tucked in the tree.

Yazen   That one's for you.

Noura   Mmm.

She takes her iPhone from him and looks at the time.

Okay, come, we're late already.

Yazen   Can't we stay home? Just us?

Noura   No.

Yazen   I don't want to go to church. For three hours.

Noura   Yazen.

Yazen But can I sleep in bed with you and Dad tonight? For Christmas?

Noura Yazen, you are a giant. And you kick.

Yazen And I definitely don't want you to be grumpy on Christmas.

Noura Definitely not grumpy.

She gets up.

Okay, *yellah*.

Yazen No. I'm not. I just, I don't want to do the pageant.

Noura I don't know why the kids have to be there so early. Are they doing a rehearsal?

Yazen I couldn't find my costume, it's not where I put it.

She goes to get his costume.

Noura I ironed it. You had it in a pile of gym clothes.

She helps him put it on over his street clothes.

Yazen Mom, I can do it.

Noura Which one are you?

Yazen The one bringing frankincense.

Noura But what's his name?

Yazen I don't know, I forgot. It doesn't matter.

Noura It matters.

Yazen Mom. Don't get too into this. Okay. We are not going to break out in Aramaic. All I say is: Behold the baby. I bring you frankincense—

She analyzes him.

Noura Well, I don't like your costume. You look like a Disney movie. Not a Chaldean King.

She takes out a keffeya/shem'magh, her father's, from amongst the presents under the tree. **Yazen** *opens the present.*

Yazen Oh, Mom, you do it.

Noura *begins to wrap his headdress.*

Noura You.

My father.

My father's father.

My father's, father's, father . . .

An eye to protect you.

She pins a gold amulet on him.

Yazen Mom, why do you hate PlayStation?

Noura I don't hate it, Yazen. I don't like violence. I don't wish that for you.

Yazen It's fantasy /

Noura To you it's fantasy. I carried a gun.

To work. In my purse, in the car. It's an awful feeling. Guns don't make you strong they make you paranoid.

Yazen Of what?

Beat.

Noura You look like a king, Yazen!

Yazen Alex.

Noura Alex, you look like my dad, your *jidu*.

Yazen Did *jidu* carry a gun?

Noura Never. Never.

Yazen I won't either, Mom.

He wields his frankincense like a lightsaber.

Frankincense power!

Noura Okay quick, outside. I need to get ready.

He runs into her, hugging her tightly.

Noura My sweet boy. My everything boy. *Yellah.*

There is no more time. She grabs her purse, her rosary; in an attempt to be more festive she quickly puts on heels or lipstick. Before she leaves, she looks back at her space. The set grows, it breathes, it changes somehow. Maybe we see elements of what the house could become, in **Noura***'s imagination. Or how it holds her memories of Mosul, Christmas dinners, a table full of family. Perhaps she touches the marble slab on the table. Then exits. The set continues to breathe. Perhaps the song we heard earlier comes back in full, an Aramaic lullaby said to have been sung by Mary to baby Jesus.*

Scene Eight

A light suddenly goes on. **Rafa'a, Noura,** *and* **Yazen** *return home from Midnight Mass. Three a.m.* **Yazen** *grabs a tin of cookies and makes for his bedroom.* **Noura** *motions for him to eat at the table instead. She prepares tea. Gathers food.*

Noura There's *pacha* in the oven.

Rafa'a Finally!

Yazen Mom.

Noura You liked it last year.

Yazen I can't face intestines at three in the morning.

Noura To break your fast, you need meat.

Yazen Jesus, Mom! Nobody fasts on Christmas Eve! Can't you be American for once?!

Rafa'a Hey /

Noura It's late. He's starving.

They watch him eat.

Rafa'a You make a good king, Yazen. Very believable.

Care to share one? Wise man?

Yazen *shares one cookie.*

Rafa'a The only other time I've been in a church, I think I was fifteen. The year your grandfather said I couldn't eat *pacha* unless I fasted and went to Christmas mass first. He said it wouldn't taste right.

Noura It does taste better when you're starving. And cold.

(*To* **Yazen**.) Okay, you can go.

Yazen *exits to his room taking the tin of cookies.*

Tareq won't eat it either.

Rafa'a He's Baghdadi.

Silence.

You and I are from Mosul. We are wired to hang on.

Noura Are we wired to hang on?

She removes a precious amulet from around her neck; she kisses it then begins wrapping it.

Rafa'a Oh.

Noura Yazen will be upset I'm not wearing it.

Rafa'a For Maryam?

Noura It's a charm for girls. For protection. I'm not a girl anymore.

She then tucks the wrapped amulet into a branch of the Christmas tree.

Rafa'a Have you prepared them for tomorrow?

Beat.

Why not?

Noura She might not come. In fact, she probably won't come at all.

Rafa'a Of course she'll come. She'll come for the food.

Noura It's three a.m. I haven't heard from her. God knows where she is, with her "friend." She left angry. Shocked that I was shocked.

Rafa'a How bad were you?

Noura Just shocked, embarrassed. She was raised by the most courageous nuns for God sakes. They defended her with their life. How could she be so proud? Like she owes nobody. She has no right to behave this way. I paid for her to come—

Looking at her phone.

She hasn't texted, she said she would, but she hasn't.

Rafa'a I've never heard you bitter.

Noura Bitter / I'm not bitter.

Rafa'a How long have we known each other? I knew your father / better than my own.

Noura You don't need to even / say it.

Rafa'a I do. I'm worried about you.

Noura It's new, I just saw her for the first time.

Rafa'a And you're gonna let her walk in here tomorrow and not tell Tareq just see what he does? That's not fair to her. To any of us.

Noura Tell him what? That she's—what? Make him crazy? I need her to come.

Rafa'a I know.

Noura What do you know?

Beat.

Rafa'a You need to let go. You need to pick up your tennis racket and hit some balls.

Noura I've already let go. You came here a long time ago, Rafa'a, with your wealth. I came here with nothing. The charities dressed me, like a child, chose my furniture, my apartment. And I had to be grateful and forget.

Rafa'a Yes, but now you built your own life. This is / you

Noura It's not just Maryam. I am trying to hold one small piece of my past together. If I let go it dies / with me.

Rafa'a There is no going back, Noura.

You can live amongst Arabs, or Christians, or Iraqis anywhere in the world it will never be the community it was, not again / so

Noura Don't you feel a great loss?

Rafa'a Yes! You used to be an architect who loved flamenco dance and the Gypsy Kings. Now, just last week in fact, I heard you tell Fresh Direct you were a Christian, immigrant from Iraq.

Noura Because they hear my accent they want to know where I'm from. Not what music I like.

Rafa'a I'm just saying if you want to hold on to what Iraq was, maybe you need to remember who you were.

Noura Who was I?

Beat. **Rafa'a** *looks at her.*

Noura I still smoke. When nobody's looking I smoke.

Rafa'a I know.

Noura It's what I do for me. And only me.

Rafa'a I won't say anything.

Noura Come on, you're a doctor. Why not lecture me on smoking rather than my obsession with my dying identity?

Rafa'a They're the same. As a Muslim, I feel it too, maybe more.

You think Muslims are okay with what's happening? Look at us. We all took part. Iraq had a chance—we fought for ourselves, not each other. Nobody survived. Let it go, Noura. How we grew up, is never coming back.

Noura Would you defend nothing? My grandfathers were Al Naqqar, they carved half of Mosul. 1800-year-old churches, all Mouslawi marble now blown / up

Rafa'a What, then, you want to carve out a Christian territory in the Nineveh plains?

Noura Well.

Rafa'a Really? Noura! What does isolation get you?

Noura Safety, space . . .

Rafa'a So you won't live with Muslims now too?

Noura My people were driven out! We're the original / Iraqis.

Rafa'a Original what? They burned my books too, Noura. Mosul wasn't hell only for Christians / look at it now

Noura Why can't you admit, there was a genocide in our hometown! / My people.

Rafa'a Noura! The baby that came in the cab this morning? You know why? Because the father wouldn't get his wife to the hospital on time. He delayed, and delayed, because I was the doctor on call—he didn't want a Muslim to be the first to touch his son.

It's everywhere, Noura. It's not how we grew up. But, I'm telling you, it's everywhere like an infection. There is no safe space. Are you telling me we have to be careful now too? Go back to our tribes?

A hundred people used to visit your father on Christmas. Christian and Muslim neighbors, not just family. Eid, you came to our house, Christmas I came to yours.

Look who's here tomorrow: myself and Maryam, one Muslim and one pregnant, Christian refugee. Maybe New York is the one place we can still celebrate together!

Noura Not for long.

Rafa'a Forget about *pacha*, mountains of *kibbi*, *dolma* / weeks of preparations

Noura You love it. It's the only reason you've been showing up for Christmas / your entire life.

Rafa'a I also wouldn't care if we went out to dinner. Because as good as the food might be I am really just here to see you.

Noura Of course the people are the / most important

Rafa'a You didn't hear me. How this fills me is not a kind of full that food can provide. Our bodies can survive on nuts. We can't be human without compassion. And this is one of the many things you give me. Radical hope and forgiveness.

Noura What do you mean?

Rafa'a Do you believe any of it, Noura?

Noura Believe what exactly?

Rafa'a Being saved. That there is a force so loving, so merciful that any harm done in this life could be forgiven.

I think a lot about this. Childbirth can be very forgiving.

Isn't forgiveness the most radical part of Christianity?

Noura Forgiveness?

Rafa'a Yes. Noura, you could just forgive her.

Noura For what? Maryam? For being pregnant?

Rafa'a For not having tea with you.

Forgive her inability to see how much you need to love her.

Noura *dissolves.*

Noura What do you know?

Rafa'a Can you simply speak it, Noura?

Endless silence. He waits for her to speak.

Noura How?

Rafa'a Like this, I'll show you—

Beat.

I've loved *once*, Noura.

I was silent too because I thought, in our circumstances, it would be dishonorable. I simply never told her.

Noura You protected her.

Rafa'a We grew up in each other's houses. I would never have asked her to convert to Islam. She would have been rejected by her family.

Noura Yes. Do you regret?

Rafa'a It's not regret. But I'll never forgive myself.

Noura For not marrying?

Rafa'a No, for my silence.

Noura Why? Why was silence the wrong choice?

Rafa'a Because silence burns the heart. It doesn't give faith or forgiveness a chance to work.

He waits for her to speak.

Noura I do need to pick up my tennis racket / and

Rafa'a All these years in America and I can't talk straight with you. I'm still stifled. What keeps me from speaking? At my age?

Noura Maybe the desperation of love lessens in middle age as you grow older?

Rafa'a It doesn't lessen.

Noura We've never spoken like this before. Aren't you afraid of what could come?

Rafa'a How do you mean?

Noura In letting go of the burden of silence—you open a door. Or maybe you close a door. Either way it's a place from which you never return.

Rafa'a "Truth is a pathless land."

Noura Who said that? I've heard it before.

Rafa'a Guess.

Noura Gandhi? Dalai Lama?

Rafa'a Krishnamurti. You loaned me the book.

Noura You took it off my table!

Rafa'a You said you loved the book.

Noura Well.

Rafa'a That's why I read it. It made for longer talks.

Beat. He offers her his hand.

Forgive me.

Noura Rafa'a, I'm so afraid she won't come.

Rafa'a Why?

Could she take his hand? She moves away instead.

Noura   I'm the one that needs forgiveness.

Tareq *enters from work with two five-pound bags of flour.*

Tareq   Four in the morning? This is crazy. We can't all be exhausted tomorrow.

Rafa'a *begins to gather his coat.*

Noura   We've been waiting. It's time for *pacha*. Scotch or tea?

Tareq   Nothing. Only my pillow! I won't lie, I broke my fast with a Reuben sandwich! I have to sleep. I want to be ready for Yazen early. Goodnight, my friend, see you tomorrow.

Rafa'a   Tomorrow.

Both men leave at the same time. **Noura** *is left alone.*

Quietly, from off stage:

Tareq   Noura, I feel the cold from here.

Noura   I know. Rafa'a left the door open.

Tareq   Why?

Noura   For the Christ child to come.

Tareq   How long? Until Christ comes?

She steps outside. She lights a cigarette.

Noura   Tareq?

Noura, *constructing in her mind, even while the foundations of her world shift.*

Are you awake? I want to talk.

What happens to the set around her?

Tareq?

She finishes the entire cigarette then walks back inside into:

Scene Nine

Christmas Day pre-dinner:

Christmas wrapping is littered around the tree. The aftermath of **Yazen** *opening a few presents.* **Noura**, **Yazen**, *and* **Tareq** *busy preparing.* **Tareq** *has stuffed a chicken,* **Yazen** *is rolling dolmas, getting ready for the big Christmas dinner.* **Tareq** *is infinitely more comfortable and in charge with food. He comes alive in a unique way while cooking. He hums along to Arabic Christmas music with the radio.* **Noura** *checks her phone often.*

Tareq   How many years has Rafa'a come for Christmas?

Noura Since I can remember. Since I was three.

Tareq He wasn't sick yesterday.

Noura *grabs her phone. Looking for a message.*

Yazen Rafa'a's sick?!

Noura He didn't text. He texted you?

Tareq An hour ago.

Noura Why? What is it?

Tareq He's not coming. But it would have to be serious for him not to come. A tradition as old as that.

Noura He has to come.

She checks through her phone again. Frustration.

I've left Maryam three messages. Nothing. But she's posted on Facebook.

Tareq *Habibti*, if it's just us it's okay.

Noura *changes the station from Christmas music to Arabic Christian programming. Loud coverage of latest ISIS atrocities blares into the room.*

Tareq Please, turn it off, I can't stand this propaganda / not on Christmas

Noura They're the only ones praying for the refugees / today.

Tareq Nora, that channel's not even Iraqi, it's evangelical, out of Texas.

Noura You don't care? How many in Erbil, trapped in malls, freezing / on Christmas?

Tareq Of course I care, but can't I have a day? My whole year is saving other people's lives. I would like a chance to live mine / for once.

Noura *checks her phone again.*

Tareq She said she was coming three weeks ago. Why are you so worried?

Noura All this effort to be together / now nobody's

Tareq We're together! It's Christmas, if it's the three of us who cares?

Noura Look at the *dolma*.

Tareq His *dolma*'s fine, Alex is doing great.

Noura He doesn't like *dolma*, so he's sloppy, like he doesn't care / to do it correctly.

Yazen I'm not sloppy / I just

Noura I want to be capable of one tradition.

Tareq We're capable. You're capable.

Noura Then where is she?

Tareq I just don't know?

Noura Fucking ISIS!

Tareq What are you talking / about?

Noura They ruin everything.

Tareq Alex. To your room.

Noura Yazen, you have to listen, it's your country, you come from these people. Yazen / come.

Tareq We are not these / people.

Noura Yazen, you have to know what's really happening.

Tareq No. This has nothing to do with Yazen.

Noura Did we defend each other? Did we speak up? No! Now everything is gone. Why can nobody admit we did this to ourselves?!

Yazen Mom.

Tareq Nora, stop. You can't compare those psychopaths to the rest / of us

Noura We're the same! Animals fighting for a place to belong and our survival depends on us destroying the people we know. *Joeh'reen'na, Aou'jat'na, Adh'falna!*

Yazen *escapes to his room.*

Tareq How are we the same? Nora, you would feed a dog before you fed yourself. Numi? We only cook like this once a year, don't destroy / dinner

Noura *Hi Khethbeh.* We've spent a month preparing to cook the Mosulawi way, so it won't be lost, on who? How many have we lost because we cannot accept who they are? I'm sick, *Anni Khalsani.*

She lets go, dropping a massive platter of food.

Tareq Noura, *Ya Thoula*! The waste. Keep yourself together.

Noura It's not Nineveh! It's not history for God sakes! Yazen wants pizza—let's order pizza!

Tareq Why is it all or nothing with you? That's exactly what they want. For you to feel helpless. I've been cooking for three weeks, now you're throwing all our hard work away because of what?

Noura We did it this way when every neighbor was stopping by, no presents, just a parade of love! Today we have nobody. Nobody.

Tareq Numi. Iraq is not over. Muslims all over Baghdad are lining bridges with Christmas lights in solidarity.

Noura And what are we doing? In solidarity?

Tareq Trying to celebrate our holiday as a family. Celebrate the citizenship we waited for, for eight years, our new lives.

Noura Congratulations, Tim, on becoming an American—Congratulations, Alex, good job! We're American now! What, we're "safe" because we're Christian? Is that why they let us in? So easily? Changing our names, is a lie—

Tareq Working at Subway sandwich? You supporting me while I took the boards, this was easy? You can still have your career, Noura, I can't. I can never return to surgery, my hands shaking. Fuck it. What's wrong with feeling safe? I'm grateful there's a place we can reinvent ourselves, a place we can forget.

Noura I don't want to forget! I'm trying desperately to remember who the hell I am.

You think they are so easy on Muslims? The people at immigration? I hated their questions. If I were dark, they would have asked me.

Tareq Asked you what?

Noura If I hurt somebody! If I did anything wrong. They only asked if I had been raped. They looked so sorry for me, a Christian, Iraqi, a white woman. They never asked what part I played in fucking up my own country.

Beat.

Tareq (*a genuine question*)   What part did you play Noura?

She takes a breath. Arabic whispers rush into the room. It's now.

The door buzzer rings.

Maryam *and* **Rafa'a** *enter.* **Rafa'a** *wears the same clothes from last night, now disheveled.*

Scene Ten

Noura My God! You came! Thank you. Thank you!

She kisses **Maryam**.

Tareq The mess, I'm so sorry / We were just

Noura (*to* **Maryam**)   Tareq, this is Tareq my husband. Rafa'a, our dear friend.

Maryam Yes. (*To* **Tareq**.) Pleasure to meet you.

She goes to shake **Tareq**'s *hand. Throughout,* **Noura** *attempts to clean the mess and set the table.*

Tareq You're from Mosul?

He doesn't shake her hand, instead **Tareq** *kisses her three times, the Iraqi way.*

Noura Yazen! Come meet Maryam!

Rafa'a (*to* **Tariq**)   I'm from Mosul too.

Rafa'a *teasingly kisses* **Tareq** *the Iraqi way.*

Rafa'a (*to* **Maryam**)   We're very happy you came.

Rafa'a *shakes* **Maryam**'*s hand.*

Maryam   Rafa'a?

Rafa'a   Yes.

Maryam   You're Muslim.

Beat.

Rafa'a   You need me to register?

Noura   We grew up together.

Maryam   What's your family name?

Beat.

Rafa'a   Noura said you were at university there in physics—did you know Dr. Shaheen?

Maryam   Of course he was a fixture, famous.

Rafa'a   He was my mentor.

Tareq   Your family how are they?

Maryam   I don't have family, I was raised at the convent / St. Georges.

Tareq   Oh of course, of course, Nora said. When did you leave?

Maryam   When the neighbors burned the convent and killed the head mother.

Silence.

Yazen *enters.*

Yazen   Maryam!

Tareq   Our son, Alex.   **Noura**   Yazen!

Yazen   I've heard so much about you.

Maryam   I've heard a lot about you, too.

Yazen   We waited to open your presents.

Tareq   Come, may I take your coat?

Maryam   Yes. Sorry I am empty handed I dropped by yesterday with presents.

She takes off her coat, again revealing her pregnancy.

Tareq   Oh wow! Okay.

Maryam (*to* **Noura**)   You didn't tell them?

Beat.

Noura No.

Maryam Okay. I'm pregnant, six months. I don't know the sex. I wanted it to be a surprise.

Tareq I'm surprised.

Maryam I'm not married. I'm still in school. I wanted the baby. I was not coerced or raped. I am really excited about being a mom and having this child. I don't need you to find me a husband. Hope that addresses all your questions. I already have a job offer so I will be able to support the child during and after my schooling—

Rafa'a Terrific, what's the job?

Maryam With the Department of Defense. I build weapons contracts.

Yazen Cool! Do you like PlayStation?

Maraym I'm mean at Minecraft.

Yazen Want to play?

Maryam Of course. (*On their way out.*) You want me to call you Yazen or Alex?

Maryam *and* **Yazen** *exit together.*

Tareq This is the Iraqi orphan we saved from ISIS?

Noura We are paying only her rooming fees. She got a full scholarship for school—we paid for her flight and room, through the church.

Tareq So I'm paying for the college bed she sleeps around in, like American sluts do?

Noura Actually, I paid for her flight and dorm fees. She is in an all-female dorm.

Tareq Well, if she has a job working for Halliburton, let's stop paying for her fucking bed.

Noura I need this dinner, please, be generous. You know nothing about what she's been through, I want you to know her.

Silence. **Tareq** *pours himself a drink.* **Noura** *begins to bring food to the table for dinner. As* **Noura** *goes in and out, the men steal moments of privacy.*

Tareq Where were you an hour ago? What, you never went home?

Rafa'a I went home.

Tareq But not to bed?

Rafa'a Sometimes I can't sleep.

Tareq You didn't go drinking, did you?

Rafa'a I don't drink.

Tareq I know you don't. That's why I asked.

Noura *enters.*

Noura (*to* **Rafa'a**) What have you been asking me to make you for the last eight years? That not a single New York bakery will make?

She exits.

Tareq Shall I get you a fresh shirt?

Beat.

What happened to you?

Rafa'a I think I should make a move.

Tareq What? Your O.B. practice is one / of the best.

Rafa'a Move cities, not careers.

Tareq London?

Rafa'a No.

Noura *enters carrying a plate of fresh bread.*

Noura *Samoon*! / Merry Christmas, Rafa'a.

Rafa'a My God! Would you look at that, she finally made *samoon*!

Noura Last night. I didn't know what to do. I made bread.

Tareq A perfect Christmas / present.

Yazen Yeah, I had five for breakfast.

Maryam *Samoon*?!

Noura There are other things. We made other things

Yazen Like "face."

Noura Tareq?

Beat.

Tareq Maryam, would you like to sit down? *Et'fadh'ahlee.*

He offers **Maryam** *a seat at the dinner table. She accepts.*

Maryam *Samoon* is the one thing I miss.

Noura I want you to feel at home. There's *Kubba Halmud, Kubba Mosul, Macloubi,* chicken / biryani

Yazen And lamb "face."

Rafa'a No *dolma*?

Noura I had *dolma* but /

Tareq Food fight!

Noura I dropped it.

Maryam This looks, smells, wow!

Rafa'a It's not Christmas without / *dolma*.

Tareq Maryam, in New York people just go to restaurants on Christmas.

Yazen Dad, that's not true.

Tareq It's true, they don't do what we do.

Yazen Jackie's mom cooks more than this.

Tareq How do you know?

Yazen I've eaten the leftovers at her house. It goes on forever.

Rafa'a Sparkling cider for us. (*He pours for* **Yazen**.) Maryam? Sparkling juice?

Noura For me too please. Yazen, why don't you pass Maryam the chicken first.

Yazen *picks up a single drumstick with his fingers and puts it on* **Maryam**'s *plate.*

Rafa'a Don't put so much on her plate, you'll scare her.

Tareq She looks starving. We have *pacha* and for our guest of honor—

He approaches her with an entire pot of lamb / pacha, a cooked head, "face" on top.

Maryam Oh God, are you really going to offer me the head like back home?

Tareq I insist, *pacha/* you have to have

Yazen No dad, don't give her the face dad.

Tareq *and* **Maryam** *go back and forth in Arabic.* "Beh'el'afiah/La." **Tareq** *offering,* **Maryam** *declining.* "Mah'Aq'der, Sud'deq Ma'aq'der, Ani Hamel." *Everyone is loading* **Maryam**'s *plate with food.*

Noura Tareq!

Tareq Okay, no "face."

Beat.

Maryam I'm so curious, you speak mostly English, in the house?

Noura Tareq insisted when we first moved.

Tareq For Alex.

Yazen So I wouldn't grow up sounding like a foreigner, now they only speak Arabic when they're telling secrets.

Tareq Or keeping secrets.

Noura Sorry, it's hot. New York apartments are hotter than Baghdad.

Rafa'a What kind of secrets do they tell, Yazen?

Noura Yazen, look the snow started.

Tareq So, Maryam, do you know who the father is?

Silence.

Noura *makes the sign of the cross, blessing dinner. But, instead of prayer, it's suddenly a tarantella of sound.*

Maryam Does it matter?

Noura The girl's alive. Isn't that / enough?

Maryam I never had a father. I'm what everyone's afraid / of.

Yazen Afraid of *you*?

Maryam (*to* **Yazen**) Yes. A woman without a guardian. I'm un-restrainable.

Rafa'a Why isn't everyone doing it, having a baby?!

Tareq Then get married.

Rafa'a I might simply father.

Maryam Exactly.

Tareq Why are you so afraid of / marriage?

Maryam (*to* **Rafa'a**) What's your work?

Rafa'a Obstetrics.

Maryam A doctor. Then they'll let you make decisions for yourself.

Rafa'a And not you?

Maryam Everywhere I go I'm just a scandal.

Yazen I want to sit next to Maryam.

Tareq Alone it's hard, even with two parents / it's hard.

Maryam I didn't have parents.

Tareq Didn't you have twenty mothers, sisters, whatever? No one's alone looking after children in Iraq. Here, you'll pay a college tuition / just for day care.

Noura Together we couldn't afford day care in New York / I tutored

Tareq She had to stop work and tutor from the house, to be with Yazen. Maternal benefits were better under Saddam / than here.

Rafa'a Oh my God, are we praising Saddam / now?

Tareq I work in the E.R. I see how this country works. It's not as charitable / as you think.

Maryam I don't want charity.

Tareq Is the father going to take responsibility?

Maryam Why?

Tareq Does he even know?

Maryam No.

Tareq Oh my God, you didn't tell him?

Maryam It wasn't easy to get pregnant.

Tareq What's that supposed to mean? It wasn't fun?

Maryam It took months for it to work, then it took months to get rid of him.

Silence.

Yazen We could be in our game killing creepers.

Maryam Right, Alex.

Noura It's the language! This dinner in Arabic how different would it be? Circling each other for hours. Gossip thickening underneath each word. In Arabic we wait, we dance, but English doesn't dance, it flies like an arrow.

Tareq Yazen, the wine / please.

Rafa'a This country will make you forget. Make you move / on.

Tareq Yazen . . .   **Noura** It makes me hold on. Maryam, I've been here eight years, still every time I close my eyes I see / violence

Tareq She wants to relive / going over

Noura Like I'm still trying to protect / the people

Tareq Who? You don't have family left there to protect.

Noura She's alive! She was with my aunt when she was killed. And she survived. We're the only people who survived exactly the same thing. And we're finally together. Who else could possibly understand what we've seen?

Tareq *Habibti*, then let's celebrate /

Noura I am celebrating Maryam.

(*To* **Maryam**.) I understand your need for life. Not outside you like an opportunity—inside you, building lungs, building feet, eyes. You needed to make life. Because everything else inside you is—

Maryam Yes.

Silence.

Tareq We have to have another child.

Beat.

Yazen   Even the snow is silent.

Noura   The loudest silence I have ever heard.

Yazen (*to* **Maryam**)   Did it ever snow in Mosul?

Rafa'a   It did when we were young. Not often / but

Maryam   Never.

Yazen   Have you never been sledding?

Maryam   I've never /

Yazen   Can we?

Tareq   After we eat.

Noura   Of course we'll go sledding / with Maryam after we eat!

Tareq   You know what's better than winter? Summer!

Yazen   When we go sledding, Mom likes to go behind me, never in front. Her laugh is the biggest laugh you have ever heard. And it gets bigger when she goes / down hill.

Noura *gets up to be closer to* **Maryam** *leaving the men to talk.*

Tareq (*to* **Rafa'a**)   What was the name of that beach? All-inclusive package, flight, hotel.

Yazen   For spring break?

Tareq   Just me and Mommy. (*He reaches for* **Noura**.)

Yazen   What?

Rafa'a   That's illegal.

Noura (*to* **Maryam**)   We made love during the war—it's all we could do, until Yazen was born.

Tareq   We've never been away together. My parents would rise from the grave / if I said I wanted a weekend alone with my wife.

But when we try to be intimate now—I still feel impossibly hungry in ways I can't control. Why now? They don't have words for this.

Maryam   PTSD.

Tareq   None of us had that until we came here.

Rafa'a   We had it, we didn't know it.

Yazen   We have PTSD?

Noura   No. I'm not reliving a trauma, I can question how we love. Why we mother.

Maryam Me too now. You can't think about it. Don't think about it.

Tareq What?

Maryam Back home.

At the Kurdish border, there was a woman in my tent, we fled so fast, she didn't even have shoes. I told her to sleep. Her kids running crazy all around her. We were half dead, but we were lucky. All of us, praising God we were so lucky. Finally we got water, the minute she closed her eyes, she's screaming "I left!" "I left!"

She's uncontrollable.

We're trying everything. "It's okay, Mama—you left. You're alive. Your children, look at them, everywhere, alive."

"I left Yousif!" she says. "God. God. I left Yousif in his crib. Sleeping. I forgot him. Forgot! Now they have him. *Daesh! Daesh!*"

There is no God. (*To* **Noura**.) Be glad you can close your eyes at all.

Beat.

Yazen She left her son?

Silence.

Rafa'a We thought it was hell before—

Noura I left. I just left.

Tareq ISIS is a different kind / of awful.

Maryam They're not "ISIS," they're Iraqis!

Tareq They're worse, you know they're worse, Iraq never used / to be

Maryam I don't know what Iraq you're talking about! Everyone's out for themselves, they profit from fear!

Tareq *stands.*

Tareq I feel like dancing. Enough sitting. (*A pop song comes to mind.*) "Shake it off. I shake it off. Shake it / off. I shake it."

Rafa'a It's why most of us left.

Maryam When did you leave?

Rafa'a I became irrelevant. A man delivering babies? I was suddenly taboo.

Maryam But when?

Rafa'a My grandmother was one of the first female O.B.s in Mosul. My mother was an O.B. Then me. I'm just saying, as a man there was room for me to serve. Then the people changed. The middle class turned tribal. I moved.

Tareq And now you're moving again?

Noura What?

Yazen   Moving where?

Rafa'a   California maybe?

Noura   Are you kidding?   **Yazen**   Why?   **Tareq**   Where?

Rafa'a   You know, Maryam, I tried leaving them once. They followed me across the world, my two best friends.

Noura (*to* **Rafa'a**)   Can you simply speak it, Rafa'a?

Rafa'a   Can you?

Maryam   It's in the blood now.

Tareq   What is?

Maryam   They say Iraqis, are rooted. Not anymore. Now, we're always running.

Yazen   We're rooted.   **Noura**   And we ran.

Tareq   Nora, we escaped.

Noura   No, I ran away.

Tareq (*to* **Maryam**)   She got us here, told militias at the door I was gone, packed our bags / in thirty minutes

Rafa'a   What about you, Maryam?

Maryam   I saved my own life /

Tareq   I held Yazen / she shut the door.

Rafa'a   My God!   **Yazen**   You look like my / *nanna*

Rafa'a   She's Noura at seventeen.

Tareq   Threw her gun in the glove compartment / I drove!

Maryam   Forget about / it

Yazen   Can we go sledding / now?

Maryam   I should never have told you that story, it's opened / a door—

Noura   It's now! The most beautiful Christmas we ever had. This family, my true family! What if we all stopped running? Tareq screams in his sleep, sometimes we can't even make love. Let the world know! Can it be just that? Spoken of? Rafa'a loves me / that's why he's leaving.

Tareq   God, Noura.   **Rafa'a**   Noura.

Noura   Can it all be spoken?

It took so long to get here. How many wars? Continents?
I was thinking I had to come to it whole—I didn't
we come with what we carry and it's constructed, salvaged
with what's here, with what's given—
This Christmas table is the fruit of generations of keeping alive

not just the food, it's you, your child, our child—

Did it take Mosul being destroyed to find each other at this table?
Could we have gotten here any other way?
Our survival here is stifling—walls, constant concrete—but we were blown open—
and if you stay in the emptiness just enough, a pattern comes
tangled with the old, but new, new urban tissue
a new pattern of life.

You think you come for the food, you think you're hungry
but really, it's Christmas!
It's the darkest day of the year
like Iraq—
and we come, even in the dark
we circle, believing
something can be born.

I haven't loved any of you for all that you are.
In trying to keep you alive, I forgot.
There are so many days I feel utterly extinct
I fight for what's left.
I have to stop, this once, love perfectly, this table
before we're apart, thrown again
running, running—

Silence.

Yazen Mom?

Everyone looks at **Noura**. **Noura** *steps away from the table. As far as she can get.* **Maryam** *follows her.*

Noura I don't know—

Maryam What?

Noura What did you hear?

Maryam I understand.

Noura You do? What did I say?

Maryam We're blessed. And afraid.

Noura Of what? You're not afraid of anything.

Maryam My mother died in childbirth. It's the only thing the nuns would tell me. So of course, now I'm afraid.

Noura No. That's not. You will not die. The hospitals here have everything.

Maryam This child is the only life I've ever had to hold onto!

I feel like an animal.

Now that I can finally touch what I want, I'm so afraid of death.

Noura Maryam. Birth is the most powerful pain. The only pain you are meant to feel. It is a pain you are equipped for. You are designed for. Do not try to dull it. Feel everything. Remember everything. Hear me, giving birth was my most intense joy. It's your whole body preparing you for every minute of motherhood.

Tareq *gets up from the table.*

Tareq Nora.

Rafa'a Tareq, I want to leave you all / together.

Tareq Good. Forget it.

Yazen What about Mom's present?

Rafa'a You give it to her, *Habibi*. It has to come from / you.

Tareq Nora.

Rafa'a Maryam, I'm glad I finally got to meet you.

Maryam Yes / glad to meet you.

Tareq Maryam, we'll have you for dinner again soon.

Maryam I'm—oh—yes, of / course.

Noura She barely / ate.

Rafa'a No. Don't go just cause I'm / going.

Noura We were talking.

Tareq Another time. The snow might get / worse.

Rafa'a Noura, Christmas is perfect.

Noura I'm not ready.

Tareq (*to* **Maryam**) Later this week?

Maryam Yes, the snow is coming heavily / now.

Noura Your gift! A gift for you.

She rushes to get **Maryam**'*s gift, she puts the wrapped necklace into* **Maryam**'*s hand.*

Maryam Thank you, and for dinner.   **Yazen** Why is everybody going?

Tareq It's time. Noura needs—

Does **Noura** *try to hand* **Maryam** *other presents? A bag of sweets? It's too fast. Too awkward.*

Maryam Alex, don't worry, we can keep building in our game.

Maryam *follows* **Rafa'a** *out.*

Noura Maryam.

Scene Eleven

Silence.

Tareq Alex, how about you go to your room for a bit. Do your PlayStation.

Yazen *exits.*

Silence.

Noura *goes to the table.*

Tareq Leave the mess. It's OK. Let's stay messy.

Silence.

You're right. We're not just surviving anymore. We're not dead.

Silence.

God, let's just get away together.

He stands, arms outstretched.

Let's take a dance class!

He flirts. Just a subtle movement in his shoulder suggests . . .

Anything is possible.

He suddenly remembers something.

Tareq Nora I have your gift! We all got it for you and it wasn't last minute, it took months, years of planning!

He hands her the hard drive **Yazen** *wrapped in a jewelry box.*

Something to inspire you.

She smiles. Looks at the package. So small it must be jewelry.

Noura In a minute.

She puts it down on the table.

Tareq What's eating you? I knew about Rafa'a, I don't care, I trust us. God, what's in you ready to explode? I want it. Is it in your heart? Where's my wife?

They are on the verge of something explosive and powerful.

Noura I have to have a cigarette.

It's only one. Please. Don't get on me.

She steps outside.

Tareq You really know how to kill a moment, Nora.

A long silence.

Tareq *talking to her from inside.*

Tareq I don't want you sending that *qah'beh* any more money.

Noura Let me finish this one / cigarette.

Tareq All that you did to give her a new life and she throws it away, like every American girl sleeping her way through college. Let her fend / for herself.

Noura She deserves a chance / she works hard.

Tareq She's arrogant, why are you defending her?

Noura She's bright, her professors / moved her up a year.

Tareq What does it matter how bright she is? She's not smart enough to keep her legs together. I won't support / her.

Noura We can help her, the baby. They could spend / summers here.

Tareq I don't understand you. You took it into your head you were going to save an Iraqi orphan. You've been sending money to the convent for how long now?

Noura I told you I was supporting / the education of

Tareq She wanted to get pregnant? No one was watching her for the first time in her life. Of course she doesn't know who the father is, she should have saved everyone the trouble. Most of all her tortured kid.

Noura Why can't she want a child?

Tareq When you're a twenty-year-old orphan running from medieval madmen, whisked off to an American university, the last thing you want is a burden.

Noura *brings her cigarette inside.*

Noura I've never heard you so spiteful.

Tareq She has a hold on you. I hate seeing you attached. To someone I don't trust, she could hurt you.

Noura How can this girl hurt me?

Tareq Pick another orphan to save. Fly over to the refugee camps. Three-year-old girls being sold as brides? Help a baby. Doesn't have to be this slut.

Noura Stop with that word.

Tareq We have to protect ourselves. She's a stranger. All we know about her is her behavior, not her parents, her lineage.

Noura We are not in Iraq any more fearing if we are going to get kidnapped or sold by our neighbors. Sadly, she wants nothing from me.

Tareq Then let her go.

Noura I won't.

Tareq You have to.

Noura I think she's brave / fearless.

Tareq   For sleeping around?

Noura   For keeping her child.

Tareq   By herself? Better not to be born. Her mother should have done the same.

Noura   *Shame*. I am sick of it. We are so unforgiving. It's the worst of who we are. If she is shameful I am more so.

Tareq   Stop.

Noura   We made love before we were married.

Tareq   Stop, Alex / will hear.

Noura   Are we ashamed now? Two middle-aged parents talking after twenty years of marriage? You think at his age he isn't talking with his friends about sex? They see more on their phones than I've seen my whole life.

Tareq   Stop talking, Noura.

Noura   I can't. I'm confused, by how much you seem to hate this girl, this woman who walked into our house today. So, she's pregnant, so what? It's Christmas. We can't feed a refugee? She's from Mosul, I have nothing left in all of Mosul. You work at a hospital, for God sakes everyday you help broken people, addicts, crazies, whole bodies cut open in front of you, and you can't be in the room with immorality? Because she doesn't act helpless? Or embarrassed for not being a virgin? I wasn't a virgin / and you married me.

Tareq   You were too easy. I think about it still.

Noura   I've never touched another man in my life. We were promised from seventeen. I have love letters you wrote to me when you were fifteen.

Tareq   You were supposed to reject me.

Noura   What do you mean? My father agreed to it before he died—you begged me to marry / you.

Tareq   You were supposed to reject my advances.

Noura   After we were engaged? Reject what?

Tareq   Every man is expected to try. Women are required to reject, to show the strength of their chastity.

Noura   You begged to kiss me every day. I did reject you.

Tareq   Until you didn't.

Noura   You begged to make love to me as a test? At seventeen years old I failed your morality test? Am I supposed to never be stronger than you—only in my sexual restraint?

Tareq   You've never been restrained. Not once in your life.

You don't even wait for me to make advances. It's belittling.

The way you moved was like you'd been taught. You could have faked it. No wonder I've been unable . . .

Noura Belittling?

Tareq I have never reconciled what you are. What you want.

Noura What am I?

Tareq I don't know.

God, I can hear myself, I sound awful, conservative. But when did you depend on me for anything? Do you ever need me?

You're impenetrable. Either completely silent, or digging up the darkest, I can't keep reliving.

Have I ever, once, behaved like you? The way you express yourself, you never think of the consequences.

I knew you didn't have a mother to teach you. Of course, I wanted to marry you, I was always going to marry you, but didn't everything change when we made love? You practically ran away in shame.

Noura I didn't run away.

Tareq I wanted to protect you.

Oh my God, how did we survive in Iraq? Shame around every corner. It was a long engagement, your father was dying, you went back to Mosul, I stayed in Baghdad, you were back and forth, five years, for university, your father died—it was a long engagement—and in that time I forgave / you.

Noura Forgave me what? Am I a slut if I show you any affection whatsoever?

Tareq That is not what I said.

Noura It's my true nature!

Tareq Don't make up this horrible scenario—

Noura Am I supposed to not be in love with my husband?

You didn't seem to hate it so much all these years. Making love to your wife. Now I know how disgusted you are on the inside.

Tareq That is not what I said. I love you! My God, you didn't hear me, I forgave you and I love you anyway / but

Noura But I am not honorable?

Tareq No you are not.

Silence.

Where does **Noura** *go now? Outside? How can she find the furthest corner of the space?*

Tareq You are always pushing me back there.

I encourage you to get a better job, take your A.R.E., you turn me away. I say okay, don't work, take a dance class—you refuse. Whatever I want, you want something else. Look at this place—how many years and there's still no couch?

You wanted to leave Iraq, I didn't. Now we're here, I am moving forward, you're moving, I don't know, you make no friends, only on Facebook—sometimes you're *more* Christian, *more* Iraqi. Noura, if we stayed we would be dead.

I refuse to continue to feel guilty about leaving. You lost everything, your department, your job. Death threats at the hospital, a bullet with my name on it.

I didn't want to go, but once I did, I walked away forever. And I chose to move forward, just us.

He tries to hold her.

I chose us.

He moves to kiss her, hold her.

Noura   I'm confused. You want me to kiss you back?

They are utterly honest.

I'm not honorable? After twenty years of marriage?

Tareq   I'm sorry. Everything hurts. I left too, every memory, my books, my practice, my—

This girl winds me up, she reminds / me

Noura   Of what? Of me?

Tareq   No. She reminds me how far Iraq has disintegrated. When did we become a nation of tribal, selfish, fucking individuals? It's not her sexuality. It's that she doesn't need anyone. Her idea of family is fatherless? What about the other half? Am I not a good father?

It's the most vulnerable of questions.

I'm tired of feeling ashamed for being an Arab. For being a man.

The day I changed my name. Iraq was finally behind me.

Silence.

Noura   We changed our names, to make them safe and pronounceable and relatable. We're losing too much / we're losing each other.

Tareq   You don't need me as much as I need you.

Noura   You're not wrong, I was ready, at seventeen, ready to make love and I didn't feel you testing me, I felt you loving me with a desperation, like I was your lifeline and you were mine. / I did need you.

Tareq You know what I see when I close my eyes? Body parts by the bag full. I can't tell where one limb begins and another one ends, who even belongs to which body part, we would race to match parts with charred / clothes.

Noura I knew that, I wanted to be strong / for you.

Tareq But if I saved a child's limb, they lost their parent instead. Saving is a sick negotiation.

Noura Yes, and I knew I would spend every day protecting you because you trusted me too with your virginity, your vulnerability. Tareq, I have never seen shame in that night because from it came so much. From it, what was born of / it was

Tareq Was what?

Noura Let me speak / it.

Tareq When I wake up screaming, the nightmare is you wheeled into the hospital, Yazen so new, so small in your arms. And I have to choose between my wife and my son. The hospital, the whole country whispers down my spine, "the child, you are responsible to save your son!" But in my nightmare, I am selfish. I let him die and never tell you. And a father who doesn't protect his child is a monster.

Beat.

Noura I know that nightmare.

Tareq What do you mean?

Noura You hate this girl because I love her?

Tareq Do you love her?

Noura Like a mother.

Tareq Why? You just met her.

Noura I'm attached to her.

Tareq Well, she is not attached to you.

Maryam *enters.*

Scene Twelve

Maryam Noura.

Tareq *and* **Noura** *stunned.*

Tareq Okay.

Noura *Ya Maryam!* Come in. Dear, sit. Please—

Maryam I got all the way to the subway, I didn't even feel the cold, the snow was so beautiful. Then I opened your present—

She interrupts herself, holding out a necklace in her hand.

Noura, I can't accept this.

She tries to hand **Noura** *back the necklace.*

Noura   Maryam, we can have tea now / all of us talk.

Maryam   I appreciate you're trying to do something kind for a fellow Iraqi / but

Noura   It's small, from my / mother.

Maryam   I'm not having a girl / and I don't believe

Noura   It wasn't for the baby / Maryam

Maryam   I just don't want anything to change how I relate to my child!

Noura   It was for you.

Maryam *puts the necklace firmly on the table.*

Tareq   How old are you?

Maryam   I don't even know.

Noura   She's twenty-six.

Maryam   What?

Everyone looks at **Noura**. *Deafening silence.*

Noura   You were born January, eighteen, 11:08 a.m. It was the coldest day on record in Mosul. I brushed snow from your cheek. You didn't feel the cold, even then.

Endless silence.

Maryam *goes to exit.*

Noura   You're leaving?

Maryam   Just stop! It's better if we don't talk anymore. Better for both of us.

Noura   I would like to know you /

Maryam   No.

Noura   Your child.

Maryam   Don't.

She is gone.

Scene Thirteen

Silence. Not even the sound of breathing. Nobody can speak. **Noura** *is in physical pain; she tries to stay standing.* **Tareq**, *same. The silence goes on forever. Maybe they're not going to say anything about it ever again. Then simultaneously:*

Noura You had to see her.   **Tareq** Noura.

Noura Would any of us know our own child if we passed them on the street? I thought of that every time I saw a girl. Dark, light, they were all her, all / ours.

Tareq Ours, Maryam?

Noura Yes.

Tareq God, Noura, what . . .?

Noura What kind of mother abandons her child before the milk comes in?

Tareq Noura, what did you think was going to happen today?

Noura It was a chance / to

Tareq To what?

Noura Should I have left my dying father? You? To raise her in a village somewhere? The stigma on her worse than that of an orphan? The stigma on you? I would have ruined your family.

Tareq What about today, Noura?

Noura It was her or you. Am I a monster for choosing you? The whole country whispered down my spine to give her up.

We have a daughter.

Tareq Stop. Just because it's true doesn't mean you speak it.

Noura I was sure after we were married I could bring her back. We both so wanted a girl. But the war, you insisted after Yazen, no more children.

Tareq So you kept it? Twenty-six years a secret?

Noura The nuns came and took her from my arms. I didn't even name her. I was silent. *Silent.*

Tareq I can't. You did the only thing you could do.

Noura I could have done more. Did I never think of leaving? Just take / her

Tareq Where? You did more than what's expected—most women have an abortion.

Silence.

Noura Is that what you would have wanted?

Tareq I don't know. I would have married you anyway.

Noura You pity me?

Tareq *goes to comfort her.*

Noura Stop. It makes me feel small. Don't look at me like I'm a victim.

Tareq Nobody left that country in one piece. If you need help, there is therapy, even the church, fine, you can heal / from this, Noura.

Noura I am not a victim, Tareq, I am a coward.

Tareq You couldn't help it.

Noura For how long can we blame our situation? I gave up our child. Yazen's sister.

Tareq What could / you do?

Noura You have a daughter. What do you feel?

Tareq Noura, this is acute. There isn't time right now to feel.

Noura I've just lost the one woman who could have been mine!

She wants nothing to do with a woman like me. What does that say about me?

If we were not silent, my God, what might we be?

She goes for her coat and purse.

I've never been restrained? I never think of the consequences?

Every day I worked to get her back.

To go home.

Iraq is not home anymore.

What little I carry

from as far back as Babylon

I've already given to Yazen, to Maryam

and to our grandchild, my blood, that's all that's left

the rest is gone. Gone.

Millions and millions of people are flooding out with nothing

they're leaving behind the beginning of time

leaving houses and libraries and languages older than Aramaic.

No wonder so many of us are drowning,

the responsibility is impossible to bear

it's the weight of being erased

of not belonging anymore. Anywhere.

She goes to leave. Snow begins to fall in the house. Over the furniture. The Christmas tree. Through the empty walls. She sees it clearly, like a mystic in rapture.

Oh Blessed Mary—

I'm so angry. All the time. Every day I try to do the right thing and it's wrong? Was it wrong?

I had a life! Endless love, endless cousins, neighbors, but did I ever have a private thought to wonder who *I* was? Twenty-six years I've lived in exile from myself.

Maybe it had to be violent? To wake me up?

What if America did a good thing?

Ripping us apart without thought—that was our chance—internet, cell phones, all of us, even your grandmother on Facebook looking for words to express herself! I wanted to rebuild Iraq! I wanted to be part of something! Three thousand years of culture destroyed and what did I do? Tareq?

Tareq Noura you have to move / on.

Noura How strong? How flexible to have survived together since the beginning of time, until now? Now?! A woman without a desk?

Tareq You're killing / yourself.

Noura Do we live for each other or for ourselves? I need a country in between.

Tareq What are you talking about?

Noura I don't know.

She stands on the table, reaches for the snow.

Tareq What are you doing?

Noura I don't know.

Beat.

Yazen!

Tareq Are you kidding?

Noura I don't want to take a dance class. It's not an opportunity I'm looking for. I need a sacrament, for exile. You want me to move on? I am moving on.

Tareq Not like this!

Noura Yazen!

Tareq *Ah'hebki. En'ti Mait'ta Men-El-Jou'e. Khal'lini Aw'wah'kel'ki.*

Noura I'm not hungry.

Tareq You didn't eat.

Noura I did.

Tareq I was watching you.

Noura What I need is not at the table.

Scene Thirteen

Tareq *gathers food for her fast.* **Yazen** *enters in snow pants, carrying a sled.*

Yazen   This place is a mess! Oh my God, Mom?!

Noura *gets down. Who she is meant to be necessitates leaving. But* **Yazen** *is everything. She stands between worlds, pulled to the point of breaking.*

Tareq   Yazen, do something about it for your mother!

Yazen   OK. But then, we're going sledding. The snow is NOW!

Noura   Yazen, I don't know how to tell / you what I've

Tareq   Yazen, the present / for your mother.

Yazen   Mom you didn't even open your present! It's the biggest surprise of your life!

Noura   Not now, Yazen, there's something I want to tell / you

Tareq *desperately offers* **Noura** *a plate of food.*

Tareq   I haven't seen you sit down this whole time. Will you sit please?

Noura   I can't sit.

Yazen   Mom, you look hungry, just eat so we can go /

Tareq   No one's going! Let me feed you Noura. Let me offer what I am.

Noura   Alex! There's something you need to know.

Tareq   How Noura? How?

Noura   Let me find it—

Yazen   Mom, the snow is perfect now.

Noura   I—

Silence.

I don't know how to let go and hold on at the same—

Silence.

Resolve.

Blackout

Production Notes

Al Naqqar is both Noura's surname and a reference to the profession of her grandfather and great-grandfathers. It refers to someone who excavates stones in a quarry, cutting them for use in the construction of homes and other buildings. It can also mean the art of engraving or carving of the stones themselves. Mosul is famous for a certain type of marble with which Noura's family worked as marble carvers and builders.

Tareq refers to himself as an Arab in the line, "I am tired of feeling ashamed for being an Arab, for being a man." While many Christian Iraqis of both Chaldean and Assyrian descent do not refer to themselves as ethnically Arab, some Iraqi Christians of a certain age and education who live in cosmopolitan areas considered themselves Arabized. Tariq's line is of course playing upon the tense relationship to being seen as an Arab man in contemporary America. However, with this line he is also challenging Noura's ideological relationship to her literal identity versus the more inclusive identity in which she was raised. It could also be a call to the tension between his Baghdadi Christian identity and her Mouslawi Christian identity.

It must be said that Noura and Tariq have a deep and connected marriage in which they love each other profoundly. Their marriage is knit together with an ancient sense of shared history and yet filled with a modern understanding of commitment, choice, and shared roles. This was not an arranged marriage and Tariq cannot be interpreted as repressive or misogynistic. The reveal of his innermost fears must remain fluid and vulnerable. He is in pursuit of greater intimacy with Noura and ultimately is trying to share his most honest self with her.

Glossary of Arabic Terms and Phrases

AA   Yes.

Adh'falna   Arabic for "Our babies."

Ah'hebki (feminine)   Arabic for "I love you."

Al Khansa   Literally "gazelle" in Arabic. Also, the nom de plume of a female poetess and contemporary of the Prophet Mohammad who wrote Al Muaallaqat poems (considered the best poems of the pre-Islamic era). The Prophet Mohammad enjoyed her poetry and asked her to recite her words at his gatherings. She is also known as "Umm Al Shuhada" or "Mother of Martyrs" since her poetry focuses on grief, loss, and praise of those who die in battle.

Ammu   Uncle.

Ani Hamel   Arabic for "I'm pregnant."

Anni Khalsani   Arabic for "I'm done" or "I'm sick."

Aou'jat'na   Arabic for "Our streets."

Baba   Father.

Beh'el'afiah   Arabic for "You're welcome."

Bismullah. Il Rahman al Rahim.   Arabic for "In the name of God, the Merciful, the Compassionate." It is the opening phrase in the first chapter of the Holy Quran.

Chal Chal   A verb in Iraqi dialect (*kalkala* in classical Arabic) meaning "to engulf."

Che Mali Wali   A traditional Iraqi song whose title is translated as "Because I Have no Ruler/Protector."

Claecha/Ek'leecha   Traditional Iraqi cookies with date filling made during the holidays.

Dolma/Doul'mah   Rice stuffed vegetables including onion skins and vine leaves.

Elhamdullah ya binti   Arabic for "Thank God, my daughter." Can be said to a relative or non-relative.

En'ti Mait'ta Men-El-Jou'e (feminine)   Arabic for "You're dying of hunger."

Et'fadh'ahlee   Arabic for "Do me the honor."

Ghada   Tomorrow.

Habibti/Habibti   Darling or sweetheart (male/female).

Haram   "Sin" or "forbidden." Can also used to mean "what a pity."

Ha'tha Eeb   Arabic for "It's shameful."

Hi Khethbeh   Arabic for "It's a lie."

Hisar   Embargo.

Huda   A woman's name meaning "God's way," "enlightenment," or "the way."

Il-Hamdu Lillah   "Praise be to God" or "Thank God."

Il-Mawt Yihrig Il-Glub   An Iraqi proverb meaning "Death burns the heart."

Joeh'reen'na   Arabic for "Our neighbors."

Jidu   Arabic for "Grandfather."

Kan El-Mafroudh Et'sa'qoudou El-Dhe'fil   Arabic for "She should have an abortion?"

Khal'lini Aw'wah'kel'ki (feminine)   Arabic for "Let me feed you."

Kibbi/Kib'beh/Kubba   A traditional appetizer made of ground lamb and bulgur wheat, stuffed with parsley and onion. It is shaped into an oval and fried.

Kunya   An honorific term used to refer to parents relating to their first-born son.

La   No.

La Ilaha Illa Allah   An Arabic phrase meaning "there is no God but God."

Macloubi   An "upside down" chicken and rice dish containing stewed meat, rice, and fried vegetables.

Mah'Aq'der   Arabic for "I can't."

Mashallah/Ma-Sha'Allah   Arabic phrase meaning "God has willed it." It is also used as an expression of joy, praise, or thankfulness.

Nanna   "Grandmother" or "Granny."

Nunu   Arabic word for "Baby." Also means a person full of light or happiness.

Pacha/Patcha   A traditional Iraqi dish made from sheep's head, stomach, and trotters. The parts are boiled and eaten with bread. Also known as boiled sheep's head, with the cooked sheep's head served atop the dish.

Qah'beh   Arabic pejorative for "Whore."

Qif   Stop.

Rah Ten'Qa'til   Arabic for "She'll be killed."

Sammura   A term of endearment which means "good companion" or "conversation partner."

Samoon   A popular flatbread from Iraq made with whole grains and sesame seeds.

Sheikh   A tribal elder.

Shem'magh/Keffeya   A traditional Arab scarf. "Shem'magh" is the Iraqi word for the garment.

Shlonich   "How are you?" in Iraqi dialect. Literally translated it means "what color are you?"

Shukran Arabic for "Thank you."

Sud'deq Arabic for "Honestly" or "Really."

Ta'al Come here.

Thoula Arabic for "Fool."

Tis'ah Nine.

Umm "Mother of."

Wayn Allah? "Where is God?"

Ya Waylee An Arabic lament meaning "Woe unto me."

Yabni Arabic for "My son."

Yaboo A call of tragedy or disaster.

Ya'ni "I mean."

Yellah/Yah'lla Arabic for "Come on!" or "Let's go!"

Youm Ruddi "Mother answer me."

Yumma "Mommy."

Yumma Weledi An Arabic lament meaning "Oh my little one."

Afterword: "The Things That Can't Be Said"

Heather Raffo

As an American woman with Iraqi roots, I was born at a critical moment in both nations' history. I came of age during the United States' first war with Iraq, and I became a professional playwright during their second war with Iraq. Each decade of my life brought increasing conflict between the two countries. The weight of balancing incommensurable cultures and lives influenced by violence has shaped not only how I create theater, but the way I connect to humanity. As a playwright, I've chosen to work across many borders: on national mainstages and in rural communities; with the military and in the Middle East; in institutional and immigrant environments both in the U.S. and internationally. I've dedicated my artistic life to bridge-building, exploring the great ambition of theater—creating empathy.

Yet after decades of exploration on stages across our nation, I've come to question the role of empathy itself. Creating empathy is not the same as creating value. I believe empathy allows audiences to feel for another but not always to see them as equals. Empathy often only offers a lens to look at "the other" and, at best, to open our hearts. It does not address how empathy often perpetuates power hierarchies nor does it require a true understanding of the role we play in each other's lives. I wonder if value demands more commitment from us than empathy ever could.

It is my hope, through the simple yet ambitious act of anthologizing, together these plays will come to be valued as much for what they reveal about an American identity as an Iraqi identity. To be valued as powerful theater, not political theater. And most importantly, that they offer awakenings for our shared global experience, not just an individual war experience. Put another way, I am less concerned that we empathize with the humanity of these characters, rather that we are made more human because of them.

Silence breaking is complicated

Two decades ago, in the final year of my MFA acting program, I set aside my focus on Shakespeare and went in search of plays about Iraq. The common practice of relying on classics to speak to the questions of our times wore heavily on me, and I longed for plays that were unapologetically relevant. I also longed to see Middle Eastern characters on our mainstages. The year was 1998, a full six years after America's first war with Iraq. Yet I could not find a single play in the English language with an Iraqi female protagonist. That year, I began writing *9 Parts of Desire*.

As I immersed myself in research, I came to realize I was the right mix of insider and outsider – Iraqi enough to be welcomed into the homes of Iraqi women yet outsider enough to be trusted with secrets that challenged cultural taboos. Crucially, I had to share as vulnerably of myself as I was asking Iraqis to share with me. In these years, I began to understand, as an artist and woman, the fiercely independent aspects of my American nature and the complex rhythms of my Iraqi femininity. It was the greatest awakening of my life. At the cusp of this awakening, 9/11 happened and another war with Iraq became inevitable.

While the theater struggled to find relevance after 9/11 in how it would tackle a rapidly changing national identity, my personal urgency was different—the survival of family, and my desire to create a shared cultural connection was at stake. I also questioned my role in the arts and how best to be impactful. I knew *9 Parts* offered a scope and specificity to the crisis even journalists struggled to achieve. I also knew live theater was capable of the kind of catharsis needed to shake people's view of the war and to help heal from it. What I discovered however was that, even in the American theater, there were things that could not be said.

9 Parts of Desire was turned down by nearly every theater and residency for which it was submitted. Its world premiere happened, instead, in Great Britain. The road to a U.S. premiere was harder than I could have predicted. I offer this because, from a contemporary vantage point, it is difficult to conceive of a time it would be a radical act to mount a play about the lives and loves of Iraqi women. But, in the absence of a canon of Middle Eastern American theater, the burden of proof was on me to show *9 Parts of Desire* was viable, not on the American theater to find the work of the future.

In late summer of 2004, when I was convinced New York doors would remain closed to me, a theater producer named Dave Fishelson read *9 Parts of Desire* while on a train coming back from Fire Island. I was in his office the next day and *9 Parts* opened Off Broadway, ten weeks later. He insisted the play premiere ahead of the 2004 presidential election and, in order to do so, he moved another play already slated in his season. Manhattan Ensemble Theater never returned to their original season; instead, *9 Parts* ran for nine sold-out months. Its commercial and critical success in both liberal and conservative circles allowed it to find a wide audience. *The New Yorker*'s John Lahr described it as "an example of how art can remake the world." However, the full quote goes on to say, "and eloquently name pain."[1] I believe it was this naming of pain that proved to be groundbreaking.

Soldiers wrote me from Iraq asking if they could read the play. A six-foot tall man from the Pentagon sobbed in my arms backstage repeating "he had no idea." Hundreds of people stayed for talkbacks during mid-term elections in D.C. wanting to discuss "what we should do." Military wives and mothers came to the show "to understand." The UN Ambassador for Iraq remarked that this play revealed what he'd dedicated his lifetime in diplomacy to achieve. A group of card-carrying Republicans in Cincinnati thanked me for speaking "truthfully to the real costs of war." And Iraqis across America were shaken. They had never seen themselves on stage, listened to by fellow Americans, speaking the things that can't be said.

Iraqi women emailed me from Iraq telling stories of reading *9 Parts of Desire* behind closed doors to their mothers. They asked how I could know secrets they kept, even from themselves. Young Iraqi actresses in Sulaymaniyah learned aspects of their history no longer found in Iraqi textbooks. As young women, to perform the play safely at their universities, almost half the text had to be cut.

In productions from India to Illinois and from the Kennedy Center to rural high schools, I attribute the watershed of emotion to naming a pain many didn't know they

---

1. Lahr, John. "The Fury and the Jury." *The New Yorker* 80, no. 34 (2004): 136.

carried. Whether the war touched us personally or lived only on our televisions, it became imbedded in our economy, psyche, and identity. As a college student from Nashville once told me after the show, "I'd heard of Iraq, but I never thought of them as people."

Was it an act of empathy she experienced? Countless students confide in me they recognize the characters of *9 Parts* as women much like themselves. But then what? Might there be greater value in understanding how our nations are connected and how a student from Nashville plays a role in that future? Should we even need to empathize in order to value and appreciate the role we play in each other's lives?

The United States has become part of the living history of tens of millions of Iraqi people. Iraqi youth have grown up speaking English with American accents learned from soldiers, from music, and from television. The largest, most expensive U.S. embassy anywhere in the world is in Baghdad. At 104 acres, it is like the Vatican – a small country within a country. The largest refugee crisis of our time had its roots in the violence and fracturing of Iraqi society, as did the sectarian fracturing now found across the Middle East. While the war itself may be in the past, our history together is just beginning. How do we understand the costs and weight of trauma across generations? If Iraq has been forever changed, demographically, by these traumas—what of America? Is Iraq a bellwether for America today?

I was never an avid opera goer, but having trained as an actress, I must confide, I dreamt of singing arias. The scale of sound seemed to me the most epic expression a human voice could make. So, when I was approached by Annenberg's Explore Foundation and City Opera Vancouver to write a libretto telling the story of the battle of Fallujah as witnessed by Marine Sgt. Christian Ellis, I began to consider the unique contribution opera could make toward our national narrative and how the far reaches of musical expression could best tell the story of war.

Fallujah would be the first opera about the Iraq War. From a military perspective, the two battles of Fallujah would be studied as the most historic of the Iraq War. I knew I was an unusual choice to write a military story. Even I was torn. Like *9 Parts*, I would have to share as much of my private feelings as I was asking military men and women to confide in me. Could I when I was fundamentally against this war? I had also just given birth to my son. There was an otherworldly tenderness I was trying to protect in how I raised a boy amidst the ever-present narrative of war that was a backdrop to my identity and, by proxy, his. If I was honest, this would be delicate and dangerous ground.

As the story consultant, Christian wanted me to dramatize a fictional account of a marine, an orphan, like himself, who dies in battle, risking everything to save an Iraqi boy. As Christian revealed himself to me, offering harrowing stories and deeply personal reflections, I began to hear from him how, in some ways, it was harder to be alive than to have died in Fallujah. In the weeks of conversations that followed, punctuated only by my caring for my newborn, he spoke in depth of his multiple suicide attempts since returning home from war. The boy he was trying to save was himself.

I began writing *Fallujah* in 2010, when the legacy of the Iraq War was still being defended. Yet more veterans were dying from suicide than in the wars themselves. I felt the national narrative would soon have to weigh in on a crucial dilemma at the heart of making this opera—was the ultimate narrative one of heroes who free the innocent, or was it a narrative of innocence lost?

Through my insistence, the libretto shifted from the battle of Fallujah to the harder battle of returning home. What did it say about their service? The legitimacy of the war? Or about the process of returning if more were dying from suicide than had served? I spent hours in deep conversations with military families, service men and women, and particularly combat marines. I was confided in, entrusted with stories even close family members didn't know. Yet, what can be spoken of privately is often not championed publicly. It would take five more years before the opera would be produced. The military community, the opera community, and American audiences all had to be ready for the prevailing narrative of war to change. In 2016, Long Beach Opera premiered *Fallujah* at the Armory National Guard. Championed by veterans for speaking what can't be spoken on a national stage, it brought together Department of Defense officials and Iraqi immigrants, active duty and civilians. Marines who had become part of the narrative of the opera, brought family and stood up in front of uncles, fathers, wives, and children to reveal their personal struggle with suicide.

The ancient Greeks used live theater to reintegrate veterans back into civilian life. Or perhaps, to introduce civilians into the private lives of returning veterans. What does it say about our contemporary society that we prefer to label as "political theater" work seeking profoundly personal awakenings, epiphanies, or what the Greeks valued as catharsis? In our modern landscape, the term "political" implies opposing sides. It is also a term often used to pigeonhole writers of Middle Eastern heritage, making their work appear agenda focused and less universal. How might we instead value work that seeks to inspire a deeper spiritual, civic witnessing, or reckoning from us all?

I vividly remember speaking to a Vietnam veteran who brought his son, an Iraq War veteran, to the opera. After seeing *Fallujah*, he said it was time he told his son what he experienced forty-five years ago in Vietnam. Perhaps the resonant power of Tobin Stokes's music or the otherworldly size of opera offered an outlet to both name pain and to finally reveal himself. Yet, I also find myself haunted by his forty-five years of silence.

Moral injury is a term that, once I understood, I began to see across all my work. It connected the dots between what I consider my theatrical influences (Shakespeare, Shange, Fornes, Churchill) and my own need to create a body of Middle Eastern-American work. Moral injury is a transgression of one's conscience. It describes the weight and pain when your moral judgment is in direct conflict with what is sanctioned by your culture, your commander, your upbringing, or your class. The knowledge that something you have done or witnessed or lived is counter to what you know to be just.

Might we all be attempting to balance a personal moral code with the cultural norms we live with? With climate change? Income inequality? The mass movements of populations? How will we come to find or define belonging in an increasingly globalized yet polarized world?

Noura, the final play in this anthology, was provoked by many things—from the fracturing of Iraq, to a shifting American identity; from the rise of polarizing ideologies to modern marriage and motherhood. At the explosive intersection of these issues, the characters of *Noura* attempt to balance individual needs with a search for community. I believe it is a balance with which many of us struggle, particularly now.

In many ways *Noura* is my most personal play. I never thought to write from a specifically Iraqi Christian perspective. But events in 2014 forever changed the course of my own family's history. In the Mosul of my father's youth, it was impolite to ask one's neighbor if they were Sunni or Shia. He spoke of a city where Christians, Jews, Muslims, and other communities lived together. While racism and discrimination existed, a deeper rootedness to country and land was hundreds if not thousands of years old. Iraqi Chaldean Christians, of which my family is a part, belonged to one of the most ancient melting pots of ethnic and religious diversity. Even for family members living outside, Iraq was still the home to which they would someday go back. This is no longer true. When ISIS overtook Mosul in 2014, neighbor turned against neighbor and most Christians felt Iraq was no longer a place they would ever belong.

I had nearly 100 family members living in Iraq at the start of the 2003 war; I now have just two cousins living in the country. My own vast network of family and community no longer exists in Iraq, and it will likely never come back. My family is now scattered across the world having fled as global refugees.

I admit, finally, to feeling lost myself. Uprooted even in New York, where I have lived for over twenty years, longer than I have lived anywhere else. I find myself searching for what friends and family struggle to articulate—the weight of being erased, of not belonging anymore, anywhere.

Belonging is a universal ambition. *Noura* is about characters who are not just torn between two cultures. Most immigrants are. It is about something more unspeakable. It is about the lengths one goes to survive. About a leaving of home so harrowing it might render one unrecognizable, even to oneself. Each character in *Noura* has a different threshold for what they are willing to remember, to forget, to speak, and, of course, for how long they will keep silent. Especially when silence is the mode of survival.

With Noura, you feel the inevitable; her silence will break. While the audience may be surprised at her particular secret, they understand it as both personal and global, as much about family as about nations. If neighbors don't stand up for neighbors, religions for other faiths, if parents can't protect their own children, how far will survival push us? How far will divisions go?

I find our current climate further polarizing refugee narratives—depicting them as either victims, or enemies. I wanted to write a story that wouldn't land "safely" in either camp. Noura is a woman who runs from sympathy. Some want to write off her husband as sexist, except he's also progressive. Each person in this play is modern and religious, loving and judgmental. Can we empathize with a female refugee who is visionary and problematic? Who is not satisfied with being grateful? If it is hard to sometimes empathize with characters in *Noura*, what does that say about the kind of refugee narratives we want or expect?

On the subject of silence alone, in the West we expect Middle Eastern women to be ever fighting for their voice and we love to champion them when they do. Yet Noura expresses herself freely throughout the whole play—she carries but one secret. Are Western women any different? What the #TimesUp and #MeToo movements revealed is that secrets, shame, and silence can be carried by hundreds of thousands of strong Western women too across race and class and economic opportunity.

The dilemma at the heart of *Noura* is a particularly modern quandary: do we live for each other or for ourselves? Forever pulled between rugged individualism and a search for greater community, Noura, like myself, like women everywhere, is struggling to balance both what she comes from and what she could be. Facing an impossible choice between the two, the shame Noura confronts is one where individual survival or personal potential might not uphold a more collective humanity. With this in mind, we cannot continue to say the long-term effects of America's war in Iraq are only about ISIS or a fractured Middle East. We must begin to connect the dots further, to the commodifying and polarizing of all peoples and societies, to the rise of sectarian, political, economic, racial, and gender divisions throughout the United States and beyond.

Noura, as a homeless architect, is the uprooted future of the planet. Someone capable of visionary solutions, yet drowning in the isolation of her time. She attempts to hold both vision and pain, past and future, community and a quest for self. She lives at the nexus of worlds. Yet, if she continues to hold tight to her secret, her silence will uphold a world order.

Silence breaking continues to be complicated

As this anthology goes to print, we are in the midst of an unprecedented global pandemic where the narrative again finds us pulled between connection and polarization. This anthology has allowed me to reflect on three decades of my own thoughts and theater discourse in relationship to the defining historic moments of my life. When read together, I see in the writing an increasingly urgent question about how connection is pursued in the face of ever-defining traumas. The anthology starts with a monologue play and ends with a family play. While the characters get closer to each other in proximity, the chasms facing them get more pronounced. Following multiple women, *9 Parts of Desire*, as a solo show, reveals interconnected aspects of all women, of an everywoman. Noura, on the other hand, finds herself isolated in her own family and home. What the women in *9 Parts* speak freely, Noura spends the whole play trying not to speak. To me, what once felt like plays about humans in the midst of war might end in discovering the war is within and, like Noura, we've been living in exile from ourselves.

In these pages and through these characters, we follow moments from nearly four decades of history. Those moments carry my experience as a woman, an artist, a mother, and a citizen. If I listen closely enough to the characters' concerns, and how history has borne those concerns, it is perhaps no surprise at all that we find ourselves pulled into an increasingly polarized world, yet a world on the brink of the most collective experience imaginable. One has only to look at Iraq, a far more ancient melting pot than ours, to recognize what kinds of divisions can be inflamed, when they were formally the fabric of a long and woven history. Might Iraq indeed be a bellwether for us all?

If I have any hopes for this book, it is that by placing these three plays in dialogue with each other, the urge to only empathize with "the other" and the "over there" is replaced by a greater, more necessary urge to value this work as a living conversation about the here and now.

Critical Essay: "Listening to the Soul of Rupture—and Difference in Heather Raffo's Iraqi-American Trilogy"

Dr. Maya E. Roth, Della Rosa Term Associate Professor of Theater, Georgetown University

I've been awake
for months
smelling burnt flesh.

— Philip, *Fallujah*

Silence. Not even the sound of breathing. Nobody can speak.
— Stage directions, *Noura*

At the heart of Heather Raffo's playwriting is *listening*. Listening to difference and the soul of rupture as traumas spiral across people and places. Listening to rhythm and tempo, to bodies and spirit, to live tensions between what is said and unsaid. Raffo listens as a woman of American and Iraqi descent, making art between and across cultures. Bringing keen intelligence and cross-cultural fluencies to bear, she stages complex relationships and insights from living in the shadows of war.

In her Production Notes for *9 Parts of Desire*'s first publication, the playwright-performer describes her experimentation with form: 'the pace quickens, time frames blur, and characters cut each other off mid-sentence driving the play toward a psychic civil war with the solo performer embodying the larger argument of what liberation means for each woman and for Iraq' (69). Raffo's focus on both psychic and social traumas, on the crossroads of personal and cultural/historic stakes, activates civic poetics. If her plays artfully compel virtuosity and empathic witness, they also express real-world stakes that, at times, disrupt our aesthetic experience. The psychic rippling of women's voices (and solo performance) in *9 Parts* gets jarred by the 'uncle's voice' recording, for instance, which ruptures the frame and stages three traumatic returns in the theatre. Beyond connecting wars in Iraq and 9/11, theatrically, the play stirs cross-cultural ethics and listening. *9 Parts of Desire* (2003), *Fallujah* (2011), and *Noura* (2018) listen as cultural traumas spiral across geographies, genders, and generations.

You have
our war now
inside you, like a burden, like an orphan
[. . .] you carry it in you—its lifetimes.

— Layal, *9 Parts of Desire*

And war, and war, and war has made me.

— Wissam, *Fallujah*

Three thousand years of culture destroyed and what did I do?
[. . .] I need a sacrament, for exile.

— Noura, *Noura*

Raffo's three original works for the stage—*9 Parts of Desire* (2003), *Fallujah* (2011), and *Noura* (2018)—can be imagined as an Iraqi-American trilogy. Each a compelling work, together they excavate an unfolding scenario of profoundly human and historic dimensions: a cycle of disparate everyday lives in triage due to a series of atrocities in Iraq spiraling across generations and communities, no less than borders and bodies in the "now." Harnessing her complex responses as artist and (female) citizen to a rising cascade of war, polarization, and displacement, these three works listen to the ruptured soul/s of contemporary Iraq and, too, of America.

Considered as a cycle, they stage an eloquent, moving cross-section of characters—female and male, Middle Eastern and American, Muslim, Christian, and secular—reeling from and reflecting on traumas to families, selves, and the global community. Their story arc moves across three decades of cataclysmic violence in Iraq: from the Persian Gulf War (1990–91), reverberating alongside Saddam's abuses in *9 Parts of Desire* as Americans invade Iraq in 2003; to the explosive early years of the Iraq War and American-led occupation (2003–11) in *Fallujah*, when insurgencies grew; to terror campaigns by ISIS—or Daesh, as Maryam curses in *Noura*—as they besiege Mosul in 2014.

For Raffo, this spiraling of tragedies destroyed her family's home/land: As she often describes in talkbacks, when she visited Iraq in 1993, nearly 100 family members still lived there; today, only two. While we worked on *Noura*, the churches her ancestors had built generations prior were bombed, Iraq's modern secular state and multi-religious pluralism overtaken by sectarian violence; the community that defined their lives split apart; the ancient heritage, which her plays' Iraqi mothers, especially, struggle to pass on, degraded.

If their modes of storytelling vary greatly—a one-woman show, an opera libretto, a play—the core imagery, themes, and driving questions remain the same. "What now? What now? What now?," "Who am I?," and "What role did we play in messing Iraq up?" Tellingly, these questions arise in moments within each play when characters query, or carry, their cross-generational legacies, spiraling beyond a single character. Both the Iraqi Girl and Layal, so different in personality and circumstance, ask "What now?" in a cycle of three questions in *9 Parts*; the worlds upended are social and existential, both. When Wissam, later caught in the crossfire in *Fallujah*, says (sings), "And war, and war, and war made me," we hear his unending experience of wars—its cyclic nature and epic scale.

Complex characters act as surrogates for social traumas, too, evoking many people—not unlike Layal, whose paintings stage her own body for others' experiences of degradation and yearning. In *9 Parts of Desire*, Umm Ghada tells of the day her daughter was killed with 402 others in the Amiriyya Bomb Shelter—their bodies fusing together with the walls. Now calling herself "Mother of Ghada" she honors her daughter (and whole family, killed), holding vigil and testimony. The Mother of "Tomorrow," not unlike Shatha in *Fallujah*, has lost her family/future, reworking a classical formation for tragedy. Written and premiered during a war when the U.S. chose not to count Iraqi deaths, mostly civilians, *9 Parts* cast its audiences as confidantes to Iraqi women across a religious and political spectrum, conjuring us to directly listen to their soul of rupture and resilience, as well as witness, across the Iraqi diaspora.

Fallujah too expresses psychic and social trauma as intertwined, theatricalizing an epic sense of abyss for not only Iraqis but also Americans who had served there. Based on Raffo's interviews with Christian Ellis, the first opera about the Iraq War provides a portal onto war traumas: As the flashbacks suggest, Philip is haunted by the brutal deaths of his fellow marines as well as Wissam, psychic trauma pressed by so many futures, friends and families destroyed. More distinctively Raffo threads the rising crisis for Iraqis across the play, as they must choose between fleeing and fighting. By listening to how war traumas ripple for families "at home" in Iraq and America, Raffo offers a feminist lens on war.

In signature ways, all three plays express lives and cultures unmoored by trauma—with the past spilling into the present, here into there, I into not I. *Fallujah* begins with a ghosting that layers times, cultural perspectives, and spaces. In *Noura*, if Tareq seems fully ready to move on as "Tim" and embrace their American life, hard won, still traumatic memories recur, graphic talismans of rupture: "You know what I see when I close my eyes?," he reveals to Noura, eight years into their lives in New York: "Body parts by the bagful—I can't tell where one limb begins and another one ends, who even belongs to which body parts." Indeed, images of dismembered body parts co-mingling arise in all three plays, inspired by stories Raffo has heard from doctors and survivors who tried to match charred body parts or honor the dead. In this, they make palpable the human and cultural brutalities of war people carry.

So different in their focal communities of engagement—a cross-section of nine fictionalized women of the Iraqi diaspora, inspired by hundreds of Raffo's conversations in Iraq in 1993; American vets and Iraqi refugees; her own family and Middle Eastern immigrants with whom she stays in community, including her students—the plays connect in theme, imagery, immersive research methods, and radical topicality. All also evoke spaces of traumatic memory, constellating the living and the dead—an ancient river where shoes from those killed in war are gathered; an ad-hoc memorial and blasted museum; the suicide wing of a U.S. military hospital; a road in Fallujah that erupted into a killing ground, flesh flying; refugee camps; an orphanage besieged, where the head mother was killed in front of the community before pillage. For each play, these spaces linger in memory, in bodies, in cultural memory, constellating the living and the dead. Evoked by language and our imagination more than staging, Raffo's plays center the *afterlives* of war trauma, the psychic and cultural impacts more than "dramatic events." By centering how we listen to rupture and difference, they also imagine that perhaps our public listening can steward pluralist ethics and communities of belonging, even spiritual care.

While Raffo engages realism and research, she doesn't write documentary, nor verbatim, theater. Poetic form—stanzas, music, choral rippling, ritualized actions—stewards psychic, subjective and ethical stakes. These aspects arise in the writing, integral to conception and revision. Expressive theatricality also stewards audience journeys: helping us to creatively hear and symbolically approach (perchance to exorcise and/or expose) the incomprehensibility of war, tyranny, exile, and displacement; crises of identity and cultures; gender, religious, and ethnic violence; the secret pulls of shame, like silence. Thus, *Noura* expresses the crisis of liminality—being between languages, homes, responsibilities to self, family, and the world—through sensory-rich listening and openness of space, interweaving (female) subjectivity and ineffable stakes.

In her climactic monologue near the end of the play, Noura connects her own sense of exile from herself, and precarity, to the waves of refugees leaving the Middle East; they interconnect.

> Millions and millions of people are flooding out with nothing
> they're leaving behind the beginning of time
> leaving houses and libraries and languages older than Aramaic.
> No wonder so many of us are drowning,
> the responsibility is impossible to bear
> it's the weight of being erased
> of not belonging anymore. Anywhere.
> *She goes to leave. Snow begins to fall in the house.*

In their development and staging, too, Raffo's three plays experiment with cross-cultural civic poetics.

Dramaturgically, these plays leverage rhythms of trauma and exile. All begin slowly, almost gently for audiences, and build through a series of short scenes like a fever dream. Each stages disrupted memory and dispersal of voices, body parts, characters, lines. In language, like scenes, Raffo writes shards and prisms: characters cut each other off, and themselves, mid-line—as em dashes and slash marks emblematize in *Noura*. When Raffo finds these cross-cuts and fragmentations, the piece lands its "psychic civil wars." Hence *Noura*'s dinner scene, which took years to land, works through cross-layering of silence, crescendo, overlapping lines, food rituals, and ruptured memories as characters testify across three distinct waves of Iraqi emigration to America; in performance, this works as a pluralist fugue on Iraq, America, gender, generation, immigration, and war.

In a civic and feminist mode, endings here are emphatically open, passing the torch to audiences to process unresolved tensions in the real world. "Listen." ends *Fallujah*, an injunction to hear the atrocities done and lived in order to move on, to heal. If *9 Parts* poses the degradation of Iraqi lives and cultural heritage with "Two dollars?," an unsentimental pivot to audience consumer values, *Noura* closes with an unfinished thought, passed to the audience. Caught in the live stakes of how to "move on" and "let go" at the same time, she leaves the audience hovering, too, in the tension of classic civic problematics between focus on self and community, home and public, rights and responsibilities, yet gendered female and staged as an immigrant living in America: now. True to the play's through-line and yet unsettling and unsettled, this moment (first staged at Playwrights Horizons) elicited gasps, as the lights dim in the gap between speech and breath.

Theatrically, the plays enact listening to difference and spiritual care. Casting audiences as community, the Mullaya opens *9 Parts* by conjuring shared symbolic space to honor lives lost (imagined by different shoes, sandals, boots). In its middle, the American, doubling for Raffo, intones a prayer of love for forty-six family members, named one after the other, enacting ritual and witness for lives across borders, prospective casualties of war. In *Fallujah*, Raffo frames the play cross-culturally, opening with a sweet encounter between an Iraqi boy and an American marine, still young, exploring connections across gulfs of background, fear, "sides." The script takes care of audiences, letting us practice goodbyes unsaid in the chorus to families, and gives space for (others') grief in the emotional climax of the play—both in the libretto and Tobin Stokes's score—via an intersecting lament by two mothers, one American, one Iraqi, each praying their son will live. In this, the play stewards a cross-cultural poetics of human equality, not only catharsis.

The centrality of Noura's inner life and our listening threads across the play. Her secret thoughts and prayers in Arabic swirl in the theater, via speakers, as she breathes in air at play's start, bringing us to her. This auditory space teaches us, also, that much is unsaid, preparing us to listen more subtly—to metaphors, bodies, silence. If the play maps spirited, mature debate across very different perspectives (its most direct civic poetics) Noura's spiritual arc comes in unspoken moments: tasting the snow with Maryam; when the ancient Aramaic song (that Heather chose) breathes with the space after Noura blesses the home; in her quiet nestling with Yazen; and when snow falls inside, transporting her and us. In these unexpected moments, the world expands; we garner a window into her experience. Yet also, we breathe together in the space. The play profoundly unsettles because we want peace.

* * *

> Listening to different people, sometimes especially opposing viewpoints, helps me to get to the soul of the piece.
>
> — Heather Raffo

For each original work, Raffo embeds herself in the communities about whom she writes, pursuing extensive research with others, from war refugees to scholars, translators to marines—not to make documentary or verbatim theatre, but rather to learn and live in the real-world stakes of the poetic worlds she creates. Attuned to the ethics of representation as well as artistic values, Raffo develops and tests the works with diverse artists and audiences, including ones opposed to her characters' views, "to get to the soul of the piece."

In her essay for this anthology, Raffo has spoken more about this. Elsewhere, I do too.

As her developmental dramaturge for both *Fallujah* and *Noura*, I have collaborated on and at times facilitated this keen listening and deep research at multiple stages of development: gestation, conception, writing and revision, workshop, rehearsals and revisions, framing for audiences, premieres. This iterative process takes years. Whereas many playwrights seek writing cocoons, Heather seeks community, to make theater that engages the world. In talkbacks, she relishes hearing what resonates, what unsettles, and why. When moments stir live conversation or disagreement in the audience, we know the play is onto something.

For Heather, the "soul" of the play reveals itself partly shaped by currents in the world, partly through active gestation, refined over years of writing, workshop, questions, images, and conversation with hundreds of people.

The soul of these plays lives not only in their "aboutness," but through their cross-currents and theatricality. Heather Raffo listens to make the plays and activates space for *our* listening through them.

Works cited

Raffo, Heather. *9 Parts of Desire.* Evanston, IL: Northwestern University Press, 2003.
Raffo, Heather. Interview with the author. April 20, 2017.

Annotated Timeline of the Life and Works of Heather Raffo

1970	Born in Okemos, Michigan.
1974	Visits Iraq for the first time.
1992	Graduates with Bachelor of Arts in Literature, University of Michigan.
1993	Moves to London and travels back to Iraq later that year.
1994	Moves to New York City.
1996	Begins graduate studies at The Old Globe and University of San Diego Shiley Graduate Theatre program.
1998	Begins writing what will become *9 Parts of Desire* for graduate thesis project. She graduates with Masters of Fine Arts from the University of San Diego.
1999	Moves back to New York City, begins working professionally as an actor.
2000	Begins research and writing expanding her thesis for what will become *9 Parts of Desire*.
2003	*9 Parts of Desire* premieres at the Edinburgh Fringe Festival. Later that year it moves to the Bush Theatre in London's Off West End.
2004	*9 Parts of Desire* premieres Off Broadway at Manhattan Ensemble Theater. It runs for nine months garnering many awards (Lucille Lortel Award and Susan Smith Blackburn Special Commendation—as well as Outer Critics Circle, Drama League, and Helen Hayes nominations).
2005–2006	*9 Parts of Desire* moves to the Geffen Playhouse, Berkeley Rep, Seattle Rep, and Arena Stage before being licensed nationally and internationally. Over the next decade, it goes on to play in fourteen countries and in nearly every major regional theater market in America. According to TCG it was one of the most produced plays of the 2007–08 national theater season.
2007	Originates *Sounds of Desire* with renowned Iraqi musician Amir El Saffar for Georgetown's LAB for Global Performance and Politics. *Sounds of Desire* is a concert version of *9 Parts of Desire* performed at standing mic, with live music. Heather and Amir travel to universities and art centers nationally and internationally over the next decade.
2008	Creates *Places of Pilgrimage*, a storytelling workshop that teaches participants how to transform their own personal narrative into theater. These workshops take her into diverse communities and universities across the nation and internationally.
2009	The Kennedy Center invites Raffo to perform *Sounds of Desire* for their International Arabesque Festival featuring arts from all over the Arab world. She expands the concert to feature a full band with Syrian vocalist Gaida, Lebanese oud player Hadi Eldebek, and Lebanese/Palestinian drummer Johnny Farraj.

2010–2012	Commissioned by Vancouver City Opera to write a libretto for what will become *Fallujah* with composer Tobin Stokes.
2010–2011	Serves as Artist in Residence at Vassar College where she researches and writes the opera *Fallujah*.
2011	Raffo further workshops *Fallujah* during a residency at Georgetown's LAB for Global Performance and Politics which includes members from the State Department, Department of Defense, active duty marines, veterans, and Iraqi scholars.
2012	City Opera Vancouver stages first, full working public performance of the opera *Fallujah*.
2013	*9 Parts of Desire* is performed for the first time in Iraq by students from the American University of Iraq—Sulaymaniyah. Raffo attends the performance.
2013–2014	Commissioned by University of Iowa's International Writing Program to participate in Book Wings Iraq—an exchange of original short plays between the University of Iowa and the University of Baghdad. After Raffo's play *Shelter Drills* premiered in Baghdad, she was invited to perform the play for the opening of the Kennedy Center's International Theater Festival.
2014	*Fallujah* is featured in the Kennedy Center's International Theater Festival.
2014	Invited to present works from *9 Parts of Desire*, *Fallujah*, and *Shelter Drills* at TEDMED global conference at the Kennedy Center.
2015	Further develops *Fallujah* with Andrea Assaf's Art2Action at University of Tampa in conversation with veterans and active duty military as well as students and local Iraqi community.
2013–2016	Receives a Doris Duke Grant through Epic Theatre Ensemble to take her Places of Pilgrimage workshop into the Arab American communities of New York. Over three years, she works closely with immigrant and American-born Middle Eastern women on developing their own narratives and writing in response to themes from Ibsen's *A Doll's House*. Raffo conceives of her own response through *Noura*.
2016	Receives a Doris Duke Grant through Georgetown University's LAB for Global Performance and Politics to write and develop *Noura*. *Noura* is workshopped with Middle East and refugee policy experts as well as with members of the State Department and Iraqi embassy.
2016	*Fallujah* premieres at Long Beach Opera, directed by Andreas Mitisek. *Fallujah* moves to New York City Opera in November of that year. The live opera is filmed by KCET and airs on PBS on Veterans Day. A documentary by PBS *Artbound* titled "Fallujah: Art, Healing and PTSD" was produced to accompany the opera.
2016/2017	Launches podcast performances through the organization Bridges of Understanding and Refugees Deeply featuring the personal narratives of Middle Eastern women in her Places of Pilgrimage workshop.

2017	*Noura* wins the Weissberger New Play Award and Jay Harris commission through Williamstown Theatre Festival. *Noura* receives developmental residencies and readings at the McCarter Theatre, Williamstown, Epic Theatre Ensemble, Kansas City Rep, Classic Stage Company, Noor Theatre and the Arab American National Museum.
2018	*Noura* premieres at the Shakespeare Theatre, Washington, D.C. directed by Joanna Settle and starring Raffo as Noura. In the spring of that year, it moves to The Arts Center at NYU Abu Dhabi in the United Arab Emirates. The New York City debut is at Playwrights Horizons in December 2018.
2018	Commissioned by Princeton University/McCarter Theater to write a short play on the subject of migration in response to a campus-wide, multi-year migration symposium.
2019	*Noura* wins Helen Hayes MacArthur Award for Outstanding Original New Play. Raffo receives the McKnight National Residency and Commission for work on a new play about migration and the global economy.
2019–2020	*Noura* begins regional productions in multiple theater venues including the Guthrie Theater, The Old Globe, Marin Theatre Company in association with Golden Thread Productions, Detroit Public Theatre, as well as internationally.

Bibliography

Works about Heather Raffo

A Study Guide for Heather Raffo's "Heather Raffo's 9 Parts of Desire." Gale, Cengage Learning, 2016.

Abdullah, Neval Nabil Mahmoud. "Fragmented Psyches and Devastating Testimonies: Staging the Post-Traumatic Experience in Iraq through Heather Raffo's 'Nine Parts of Desire' and Judith Thompson's 'Palace of the End'" *International Journal of Arabic-English Studies (IJAES)*, 17(2017). http://www.ijaes.net/article/FullText/6?volume=17&issue=1.

Artbound, Season 8, Episode 3, "Fallujah: Art, Healing and PTSD," directed by Matt Glass and Jordan Wayne Long, aired May 24, 2016 on KCET, https://www.kcet.org/shows/artbound/episodes/fallujah-art-healing-and-ptsd.

Awad Allah and Sahar Abdel Khalek, "Uncanny Planes of Menace in Heather Raffo's *9 Parts of Desire* (October 8, 2019)." *AWEJ for Translation & Literary Studies*, 3, no. 4. October 2019. https://ssrn.com/abstract=3483815 or http://dx.doi.org/10.2139/ssrn.3483815.

Basiouny, Dalia and Marvin Carlson. 2010. "Current Trends in Arab-American Performance" in *Performance, Exile and "America."* Edited by Yana Meerzon and Silvija Jestrovic. New York: Palgrave Macmillan.

Beach, Maria. "Reviewed Work: *Nine Parts of Desire* by Heather Raffo, Joanna Settle." *Theatre Journal* 58, no. 1 (2006): 102–103.

Beete, Paulette. "Writing the Untold Story: First Person with Actress and Playwright Heather Raffo." Art Works Blog. *National Endowment for the Arts*, March 9, 2018, https://www.arts.gov/art-works/2018/writing-untold-story-first-person-actress-and-playwright-heather-raffo.

Boliek, Mollie, Kuntz, Mark, Lortz, James, O'Reilly, Maureen E., and Western Washington University, Degree Granting Institution. *Shock and Awe: The Theatre and Dramatic Literature of September 11th*. Bellingham, WA: Western Washington University, 2010.

Books and Arts Daily. "Fallujah the Opera," hosted by Daniel Browning, aired July 18, 2012 on ABC National Radio, https://www.abc.net.au/radionational/programs/archived/booksandarts/fallujah-the-opera/4137882.

Colleran, Jeanne M. *Theatre and War: Theatrical Responses since 1991*. New York: Palgrave Macmillan, 2012.

Denyer, Heather. "Heather Raffo on *Noura*." *Arab Stages* 5, no. 1 (2016). https://arabstages.org/2016/10/heather-raffo-on-noura.

Douglas, Jennifer. "The Struggle for Transcendence: Iraqi Muslim Women in Heather Raffo's *9 Parts of Desire*." In *Muslims and American Popular Culture*, Vol. 1, *Entertainment and Digital Culture*. Santa Barbara, CA: Praeger, 2014.

El Shoura, Sherine Moustafa. "Theatrical Strategies of Testimony in Judith Thompson's *Palace and the End* and Heather Raffo's *9 Parts of Desire*." *Annals of the Faculty of Arts*, Ain Shams University, vol. 44 (January–March 2016). https://aafu.journals.ekb.eg/article_9339_d5d869c1795714e330c660fa8fd31386.pdf.

Farfan, Penny and Ferris, Lesley. *Contemporary Women Playwrights: Into the Twenty-first Century*. Basingstoke, Hampshire; New York: Palgrave Macmillan, 2013.

Friedman, Sharon. "The Gendered Terrain in Contemporary Theatre of War by Women." *Theatre Journal* 62, no. 4 (2010): 593–610.

Goldner, Liz. "Back to Iraq: 'Fallujah' Opera Reflects the Aftermath of War." KCET.ORG, May 19, 2016, https://www.kcet.org/shows/artbound/fallujah-opera-war-in-iraq-charles-annenberg-weingarten.

Green, Jesse. "Review: In 'Noura' an Iraqi Refugee Leaves More Than Home Behind." *New York Times*, December 10, 2018, Arts, https://www.nytimes.com/2018/12/10/theater/noura-review-playwrights-horizons.html.

Heidarzadegan, Nazila. *The Middle Eastern American Theatre: Negation or Negotiation of Identity: a Bhabhaian Postcolonial Reading of Three Plays*. Ankara: Akademisyen Kitabevi, 2019.

Hill, Holly and Dina A. Amin. *Salaam, Peace: An Anthology of Middle Eastern-American Drama*. 1st ed. New York: Theatre Communications Group, 2009.

Heather Raffo, interview with the author, May 19, 2010; February 20, 2020.

Long Beach Opera. *Fallujah*. Long Beach: Long Beach Opera, 2016. https://www.linktv.org/sites/kl/files/atoms/files/fallujah_opera_program_book.pdf.

Mantoan, Lindsey. "Not Just 'Over There': Theater of the Real and Iraqi Voices." *War as Performance: Conflicts in Iraq and Political Theatricality*. Cham, Switzerland: Palgrave Macmillan, 2018. https://doi.org/10.1007/978-3-319-94367-1.

Najjar, Michael Malek. *Arab American Drama, Film and Performance: A Critical Study, 1908 to the Present*. Jefferson, N.C.: McFarland & Company, Inc., 2015.

Najjar, Michael Malek. *Four Arab American Plays: Works by Leila Buck, Jamil Khoury, Yussef El Guindi, and Lameece Issaq & Jacob Kader*. Jefferson, N.C.: McFarland & Company, Inc., 2014.

Najjar, Michael Malek. *Middle Eastern American Theatre: Communities, Cultures and Artists*. London: Bloomsbury, 2021.

Nordlinger, Jay. "New York Chronicle." *New Criterion* 35, no.5 (2017): 71–74. http://search.ebscohost.com.libproxy.uoregon.edu/login.aspx?direct=true&db=aph&AN=120458138&site=ehost-live&scope=site.

Outman, Kelsey. "From Iraq to Opera: Veteran Christian Ellis's Journey to *Fallujah*." westword.com, July 2, 2012, http://blogs.westword.com/showandtell/2012/07/from_iraq_to_opera_a_veterans.php.

Playwrights Horizons. "In Process: Heather Raffo on Noura". YouTube video, 02:06. Posted November 27, 2018. https://www.youtube.com/watch?time_continue=16&v=tlXFDPUjiDQ.

Playwrights Horizons. "Noura." https://www.playwrightshorizons.org/shows/plays/noura/.

Renner, Pamela. "Iraq Through the Eyes of Its Women." *American Theatre* 22, no.4 (2005): 20–71. http://search.ebscohost.com.libproxy.uoregon.edu/login.aspx?direct=true&db=aph&AN=16560220&site=ehost-live&scope=site.

Romanska, Magda. "Trauma and Testimony: Heather Raffo's '9 Parts of Desire'." *Alif: Journal of Comparative Poetics*, no. 30 (2010): 211–239.

Saal, Ilka. "Documenting War: Theatrical Interventions by Emily Mann and Heather Raffo." In *Performing Gender Violence: Plays by Contemporary American Women Dramatists*, edited by Barbara Ozieblo and Noelia Hernando-Real, 131–154. New York: Palgrave Macmillan, 2012.

Sandler, Lauren. "An American and Her Nine Iraqi Sisters." *New York Times*, October 17, 2004, Arts, https://www.nytimes.com/2004/10/17/theater/newsandfeatures/an-american-and-her-nine-iraqi-sisters.html.

Segall, Kimberly Wedeven. *Performing Democracy in Iraq And South Africa: Gender, Media, and Resistance*. Syracuse: Syracuse University Press, 2016.

Mahadi, Tengku Sepora and Maysoon Taher Muhi. "Shahrzad Tells Her Stories in Raffo's *Nine Parts of Desire*." *International Journal of Social Sciences and Education*, 2, no. 1 (January 2012). http://ijsse.com/sites/default/files/issues/2012/volume%202%20issue%201%20Jan%202012/paper%208/paper-08.pdf.

Smith, David. "Heather Raffo: the Iraqi-American Playwright Challenging Stereotypes." *Guardian*, February 28, 2018, https://www.theguardian.com/stage/2018/feb/28/heather-raffo-interview-playwright-noura-iraq-america.

Soncini, Sara. *Forms of Conflict: Contemporary Wars on the British Stage*. Exeter Performance Studies. Exeter: University of Exeter Press, 2015.
Tolin, Lisa. "Peeling Back the Layers: Midwest Native's Play Reveals Complexity of Iraqi Women." LJWorld.com, February 10, 2005, News, https://www2.ljworld.com/news/2005/feb/10/peeling_back_the.
Ulaby, Neda. "An Iraq War Opera Finds a Vein of Empathy." npr.org, March 18, 2016, https://www.npr.org/sections/deceptivecadence/2016/03/18/470973622/an-iraq-war-opera-finds-a-vein-of-empathy.
Weinert-Kendt, Rob. "Bringing 'Desire' Home." *American Theatre* 30, no. 6 (2013): 13. http://search.ebscohost.com.libproxy.uoregon.edu/login.aspx?direct=true&db=aph&AN=88160785&site=ehost-live&scope=site.
"Women to Women: Heather Raffo, Actress, 'Nine Parts of Desire'," YouTube video, 27:43, June 8, 2011, https://www.youtube.com/watch?v=C0myV6hA6QU.

Further works by Heather Raffo

"Author's Statement" in *Salaam: Peace: An Anthology of Middle Eastern-American Drama*, 111–112. Edited by Holly Hill and Dina Amin. New York: Theatre Communications Group, 2009.
9 Parts of Desire, directed by Joanna Settle (2005; New York: Videotaped by the New York Public Library's Theatre on Film and Tape Archive at Manhattan Ensemble Theater, January 12, 2005).
9 Parts of Desire in *Salaam: Peace: An Anthology of Middle Eastern-American Drama*. Edited by Holly Hill and Dina Amin, 109–170, 113–170. New York: Theatre Communications Group, 2009.
Heather Raffo's 9 Parts of Desire: A Play. Evanston, IL: Northwestern University Press, 2006.
Heather Raffo's 9 Parts of Desire. New York: Dramatists Play Service, 2006.
"Heather Raffo's aha! moment: wait a minute—was that her city we were bombing? Where scores of her close relatives still lived? Watching a war on TV, the actress faces the gulf in her own identity." *O, The Oprah Magazine*, September 2006, 100+. Gale General OneFile http://link.galegroup.com/apps/doc/A152872582/ITOF?u=s8492775&sid=ITOF&xid=6251e7a6.
Nine Parts of Desire. London: Thebushtheatre, 2003.
Noura. Hanover, N.H.: Playwrights Horizon Preview Editions, 2018.
Noura, directed by Joanna Settle. 2018; New York: Videotaped by the New York Public Library's Theatre on Film and Tape Archive at Playwrights Horizons, New York, December 19, 2018).
"World Theatre Day Message 2018 by Heather Raffo." Tcg.org. https://www.tcg.org/International/InternationalActivities/WorldTheatreDay/History/WTD2018.aspx.

Related readings

Al-Azzawi, Souad N. "The Responsibility of the US in Contaminating Iraq with Depleted Uranium," globalresearch.ca, November 8, 2009. https://www.globalresearch.ca/the-responsibility-of-the-us-in-contaminating-iraq-with-depleted-uranium/15966.
Al-Obeidi, Muthana. "The Challenge of Return: Features of Demographic Shifts in Mosul after ISIS Defeat," *Future for Advanced Research & Studies*, July 20, 2017. https://futureuae.

com/m/Mainpage/Item/3034/the-challenge-of-return-features-of-demographic-shifts-in-mosul-after-isis-defeat/.

Coles, T.J. "Life Among the Rubble: Mosul 18 Months after 'Liberation'," *Counterpunch*, July 4, 2019. https://www.counterpunch.org/2019/07/04/life-among-the-rubble-mosul-18-months-after-liberation/.

Pontifex, John. "The End of Iraqi Christianity?" *Catholic Herald*, January 16, 2020. https://catholicherald.co.uk/the-end-of-iraqi-christianity/.

Simon, Reeva S. "Mosul." *Encyclopedia of the Modern Middle East and North Africa*, edited by Philip Mattar, 2nd ed., vol. 3, Macmillan Reference USA, 2004, p. 1582. Gale Virtual Reference Library, http://link.galegroup.com/apps/doc/CX3424601881/GVRL?u=euge94201&sid=GVRL&xid=2d41cd5a.

Wilson, Jaime. "US Admits Using White Phosphorus in Falluja." *Guardian*, November 16, 2005. https://www.theguardian.com/world/2005/nov/16/iraq.usa.

Links to performances online

Raffo, Heather. *Heather Raffo's 9 Parts of Desire*. Audiobook on CD. 2005.

Raffo, Heather. "9 Parts of Desire." SoundCloud audio, 71:19, 2005, June 7, 2020. https://soundcloud.com/user-348637583/sets/heather-raffos-iraq-plays-9-parts-of-desire

Raffo, Heather, writer and Tobin Stokes, composer. *Fallujah*. Directed by Andreas Mitisek, featuring LaMarcus Miller, Suzan Hanson, and Ani Maldjian. Aired Friday, March 18, 2016, KCETLink Media Group. https://www.kcet.org/shows/fallujah.

Lightning Source UK Ltd.
Milton Keynes UK
UKHW020120110221
378576UK00005B/61